THE
Resilient
CHURCH

The *Resilient* Church

The Glory, the Shame, & the Hope for Tomorrow

Mike Aquilina

LAMBING PRESS
PITTSBURGH, PA

Lambing Press
PO Box 23262
Pittsburgh, PA 15222
lambingpress.com

ISBN-13: 978-0692613474
ISBN-10: 0692613471

Cover design by Christina Aquilina

Made and printed in the United States of America

For Mary Agnes

*In truth, every event of this world
is a type of those that follow,
history proceeding forward
as a circle ever enlarging.*

—Venerable John Henry Newman

Contents

Introduction	7
1. The Martyr's Cup	13
2. The Case for Christianity	27
3. Heresy and Orthodoxy	39
4. Light in the Dark Ages	53
5. Crusades Abroad and at Home	67
6. Reformation Inside and Out	85
7. The Conversion of the New World	99
8. The World Goes Mad	111
9. The Secular Age	129
10. A Century of Cataclysms	143
11. The History of the Future	159
Notes	170

Introduction

History, with Arms Upraised

If we were to take a trowel, as archaeologists do, and dig down to the earliest remains of our Christian ancestors, what would we discover?

We would likely find what archaeologists have found on excavations in lands stretching from Italy and France to Syria and Egypt. On lamps and murals, on statuary and on pilgrim flasks, again and again we would see stylized fish and anchors, palm branches and grape clusters. And among the most common symbols found on these Christian artifacts would be the "orant" figure.

That figure, and its frequency in the archaeological record, speaks volumes about the history of the early Church. For whenever the early Christians wanted to depict their fellow believers—whether the heroes of biblical stories or the most ordinary churchgoer—they portrayed them the same way, as an orant. The word comes from the Latin for "person who prays." According to one scholar of ancient Christianity, "No human symbol occurs more frequently and is more vital"[1] than the orant. The testimony of the archaeological record is clear: to be a Christian is to be a person at prayer.

The orant stands upright with his feet firmly planted in this world, but his arms raised heavenward. Almost always, the figure is youthful and beardless. Sometimes, the orant is veiled, and so very likely is feminine. When the Christians painted biblical scenes, whether in their burial chambers or in their house churches, they portrayed the lead figures—such as Noah, Moses, Daniel, Susanna—in the orant pose. Most orants appear with peaceful or even smiling facial expressions, which sometimes starkly contrast with their perilous backdrop: a lion's den (Daniel), a hostile courtroom (Susanna), or imminent sacrificial death (Isaac).

The early Christians themselves left us no interpretation of the figure. They did not mention it in the sermons or letters that have survived. But historians have proposed many possible meanings. The orant, they say, is perpetually young, as a child of God. The orant is veiled and feminine, because in Scripture the Church is the bride of Christ. The orant appeals to heaven with arms upraised, because the Christian's earthly situation was dire. The orant stretches out its arms to evoke the figure of Jesus on the cross—identifying every believer as a child of God in imitation of Christ, and in Christ. We are, said the Church Fathers, "sons in the Son."[2] All of these possibilities are persuasive, and all of them square with the literary record of the ancient Church.

The orant appeared everywhere during the centuries of Roman persecution. In fact, the "person of prayer" turns up far more often in excavations than does the cross of Jesus Christ! It seems that, instead of showing Jesus in his agony, the Church chose to portray Christians in cruciform—Christians taking up the cross and lifting their arms to heaven. The orant began to vanish from Christian art only with the "peace of the Church," the legalization of Christianity in the Roman Empire.

This leads some scholars to surmise that the orant represents, very simply, a Christian in mortal peril, a Christian crying out for deliverance. But, if that is the case, then the orant should be a symbol always in season. For Christians always live amid tumult and strife.

In recent decades, tumult and strife have been constant themes in the secular media's coverage of the Church, in opinion columns in Catholic publications, and even in discussions at parish council meetings. We agonize over *the* crisis, whatever that crisis may be at the moment—the decline in church attendance, the lack of vocations, dissident theology, and all manner of scandals. To know history, however, is to know that the Church is always, in a sense, "in crisis."

This book presents a handful of episodes from Christian history. They are sketches of moments of crisis, and they illustrate how God remains faithful in every circumstance, even when his people have betrayed him and forgotten his covenant. History shows us that Christ remains constant in the fulfillment of his promises—that he would be with the Church always, until the close of the age (see Matthew 28:20), and that the gates of hell, the powers of death, would not prevail against the Church (see Matthew 16:18). Christ did not promise that Peter would not die, nor that the Church would be spared the death of its martyrs. But death would be powerless against Christ's saints, and its power would not prevail.

This book is not a chronicle or even, strictly speaking, a history. It covers only a sampling of years from just a few spots on the globe. I've tried to select the stories that enthusiasts of history have found most memorable. They are not always edifying stories, since Christians—and even Christian leaders and clergy—sometimes behave badly.

But Christian history never shrinks from these realities. At the end of the nineteenth century, Pope Leo XIII said, quoting

Cicero, "The first law of history is not to dare to utter falsehood; the second, not to fear to speak the truth."[3] At the end of the twentieth century, Pope John Paul II apologized publicly for the sins of Christians in the long-ago past. None of this should shock us. We tell the Christian story in the same way that we live our Christian lives, with a critical and repentant eye on the past, but with well-founded hope for the future. We have hope, above all, in the promises of almighty God, but also because the historical record gives us assurance of his constancy. God always delivers us—individually and collectively, as his Church—though not always in the way we wish. We would have him deliver us *from* suffering, though it is better for us to know deliverance *through* suffering, as Jesus did, when he was affixed to the cross, and fixed forever in history in the form of the orant.

Cynics often say that history is written by the victors. But that is not true of Christian history, at least in the way that cynics usually mean it. Certainly, the Church has known its moments of cultural triumph and even tremendous political influence. But those were not always the moments when the Church's members shone with great moral rectitude. Indeed, for Christians, the greater struggle seems to come in times of apparent peace, when we are prone to grow comfortable and to forget that our kingdom is not "of this world" (see John 18:36). It is at least arguable that the Church has flourished most, in spiritual terms, when it has suffered most in material terms—as at the hands of third-century pagans or twentieth-century Communists. On the other hand, the Church's greatest losses and deepest shames usually came, either directly or indirectly, as a result of the sin and treachery of its own members.

This is the inevitable course of history. The Church is the

kingdom of heaven, and until the end of time, Jesus tells us, it is sown with wheat and weeds (see Matthew 13:24-30). Listen to St. Augustine commenting on that passage from the gospel:

> While the devil is bound, the saints reign with Christ during the time between His first and second coming. For the Church could not now be called His kingdom or "the kingdom of heaven" unless His saints were even now reigning with Him. . . . And it is from the Church that the reapers shall gather the tares which He allowed to grow alongside the wheat until the harvest, as He explains: "the harvest is the close of the age, and the reapers are angels. Just as the weeds are gathered and burned with fire, so will it be at the close of the age. The Son of man will send His angels, and they will gather out of His kingdom all causes of sin and all evildoers" (Matthew 13:39-41). Can He mean that they are gathered out of the future kingdom in which there are no offenses? Of course not. Then they must be gathered out of His present kingdom, the Church. . . . So the Church even now is the kingdom of Christ and the kingdom of heaven. Even now His saints reign with Him, though in a different way than they will reign in the hereafter. And, though the tares grow alongside the wheat in the Church, they do not reign with Him. . . . In short, they reign with Him who are so in His kingdom that they themselves are His kingdom.[4]

Christians who persevere in faith are those who know, from sacred as well as secular history, that Christ's kingdom is *in* this world but not *of* this world. Until history's consummation, the kingdom belongs to those who raise their hands to heaven, whence comes their help.

And the help always arrives. It is nothing short of a miracle that the Catholic Church has survived two thousand years in spite of everything—in spite of dungeon, fire, and sword, in spite of epidemics, scandals, heresies, and defections. No other earthly institution can make the same claim. The empires of Persia, Babylon, Macedon, and Rome, of France, Spain, Britain, and Russia, have crumbled, as will all others. Yet St. Peter's barque has sailed through all the storms of history. And the Church has endured as a living and growing worldwide kingdom, always itself a reign and never a ruin. It is, indeed, the resilient Church.

In one ancient painting, the biblical Job appears in the foreground as an orant figure, his arms outstretched and his expression serene as he endures the extremes of human suffering and the bad counsel of his friends. No storm can shake his inmost calm. He knows that his redeemer lives (see Job 19:25).

Job teaches a lesson confirmed by millennia of the Church's experience. To be faithful to God means, inevitably, to suffer with Christ—in the Church and for the Church. What St. Paul said of himself could serve as the personal history of Christians and the corporate history of Catholicism: "In my flesh I am completing what is lacking in Christ's afflictions for the sake of his body, that is, the church" (Colossians 1:24). It is our privilege that Christ empowers us to suffer and save, as he himself suffered and saved, and that we do so, even now, within his kingdom and his Church.

To suffer so is to reign over history, even when history seems to crush us. ❧

1

The Martyr's Cup

In July of A.D. 64, during the tenth year of the Roman emperor Nero's reign, a great fire consumed much of the city of Rome. The fire raged out of control for seven days—and then it started again, mysteriously, a day later. Many in Rome knew that Nero had been eager to do some urban redevelopment. He had a plan that included an opulent golden palace for himself. The problem was that so many buildings were standing in his way—many of them teeming wooden tenements housing Rome's poor and working class.

The fire seemed too convenient for Nero's purposes—and his delight in watching the blaze didn't relieve anyone's suspicions. If he didn't exactly fiddle while Rome burned, he at least recited his poems. Nero needed a scapegoat, and an upstart religious cult, Jewish in origin and with foreign associations, served his purposes well. Nero, who was a perverse expert at human torment, ordered that some of its members be tortured—to the point that they would confess to any crime. Once they had confessed, he had still others arrested.

He must have known, however, that the charges would not hold up. So he condemned the Christians not for arson, or treason, or conspiracy, but for "hatred of humanity."[1]

To amuse the people, the emperor arranged for the execution of these Christians "criminals" to be a spectacle—entertainment on a grand scale. The Roman historian Tacitus (who had contempt for the new religion, but greater contempt for Nero) described in gruesome detail the tortures that took place amid a party in Nero's gardens:

> Mockery of every sort was added to their deaths. Covered with the skins of beasts, they were torn by dogs and perished, or were nailed to crosses, or were doomed to the flames. These served to illuminate the night when daylight failed. Nero had thrown open the gardens for the spectacle, and was exhibiting a show in the circus, while he mingled with the people in the costume of a charioteer or drove about in a chariot. Hence, even for criminals who deserved extreme and exemplary punishment there arose a feeling of compassion; for it was not, as it seemed, for the public good, but to glut one man's cruelty, that they were being punished.[2]

That is all we know about the first Roman martyrs. We know none of their names. Tacitus didn't tell us why they were willing to die this way rather than renounce their faith. Yet, this should be an important question for us to consider. Why did the martyrs do this? What prepared them to face death so bravely? To what exactly did they bear witness with their death?

CHRISTIAN SIGNS

The first generation of the Church was characterized by several unmistakable signs. St. Luke tells us that the first Christians, one and all, "devoted themselves to the apostles' teaching and fellowship [*koinonia*], to the breaking of bread and the prayers" (Acts 2:42).

This is a precious snapshot, because we do not know as much about those first Christians as we would like to know. They were a small group, not especially wealthy, without social or political status, and often operating underground. What's more, over the next 275 years, imperial and local governments tried fairly regularly to wipe out all traces of Christianity—destroying not only the Christians' bodies but their books and their possessions as well. What we have left are the handful of documents that survived—mostly sermons, letters, and liturgies—as well as a few other scraps of parchment or painted wood, and the shards of pottery that the desert sands have preserved for us.

Yet, what we see in those surviving documents and what we find in the archaeological digs confirm all that we learn in the Acts of the Apostles, especially the detail that the first Christians "devoted themselves to the apostles' teaching and fellowship, to the breaking of bread and the prayers" (2:42). One phrase especially—*the breaking of bread*—recurs in many of the scraps we have from those first centuries, and it always refers to the eucharistic liturgy, the Lord's Supper.

Our first Christian ancestors devoted themselves to the Eucharist, and that is perhaps the most important way they showed themselves to be Christians. No other Christian practice is so well attested to from those early years. No doctrine is so systematically worked out as the doctrine of the Eucharist.

It was when the early Christians gathered for the Eucharist that all this—their common life, their charity, their fidelity to the teaching of the apostles—happened most clearly, directly, and intensely. They experienced fellowship with each other and together heard the apostles' teaching, and they broke the bread in the accustomed way, as they said the customary prayers.

So it was in the newborn Church. The Church took its identity from its unity in belief and charity, which was sustained by the Eucharist.

EUCHARIST EVERYWHERE

Christianity spread rapidly through the Roman Empire. One modern sociologist estimates that, in the centuries that concern us here, the number of believers increased at a rate of 40 percent per decade. By the middle of the fourth century, there were thirty-three million Christians in an empire of sixty million people.[3]

That meant that the Eucharist was celebrated everywhere. And the fact that it was celebrated everywhere was itself a favorite theme of the earliest Fathers of the Church. Justin the Martyr commented in the *Dialogue with Trypho* that, by the year 150, "There is not one single race of men . . . among whom prayers and Eucharist are not offered through the name of the crucified Jesus."[4] Justin is one of many ancient fathers who applied the Old Testament prophecy of Malachi to the liturgy: "From the rising of the sun to its setting my name is great among the nations, and in every place incense is offered to my name, and a pure offering" (1:11). Those lines found their way into many eucharistic prayers, where they remain even to this day.

As the Church moved outward from Jerusalem, this is what believers did: they offered the Eucharist. The early histories tell us that when the apostle Jude established the Church in the city of Edessa, his first task was to ordain priests and to teach them to celebrate the Eucharist.

This is what the early Church was about. Everything that

was good in Christian life flowed naturally and supernaturally from that one great eucharistic reality: from the Christians' sacramental experience of fellowship and communion, of the teaching of the apostles, of the breaking of the bread, and of the prayers.

REAL MARTYRDOM

But there was another dominant reality in the ancient Church. It is something that appears just as often in the archaeological record and in the paper trail of the early Christians. That something is martyrdom. Persecution.

Martyrdom occupied the attention of the first Christians because it was always a real possibility. Shortly after Christianity arrived in the city of Rome, the emperor Nero discovered that Christians could provide an almost unlimited supply of victims for his circus spectacles. The emperors needed to keep the city's populace amused, and one way to do so was by providing spectacularly violent and bloody entertainment.

The Christians' moral code made them none too popular with their neighbors, so the pagan Romans were more than willing to cheer as the Christians were doused with pitch and set on fire, or sent into the ring to battle hungry wild animals or armed gladiators. It was all in a day's fun in ancient Rome. Over time, Nero's perverted whims settled into laws and legal precedents, as later emperors issued further rulings on the Christian problem. Outside the law, mob violence against Christians was fairly common and rarely punished.

The Christians applied a certain term to their brothers and sisters who were persecuted and killed. They called them "martyrs"—which means, literally, "witnesses in a court of law." And to the martyrs they accorded a reverence matched only by their reverence for the Eucharist.

In fact, the early Christians used the same language to describe martyrdom as they used to describe the Eucharist. We see this in the New Testament Book of Revelation, when John describes his vision of heaven. There, he saw "under the altar the souls of those who had been slaughtered for the word of God and for the testimony they had given" (6:9). There, under the altar of sacrifice, were the martyrs, the witnesses.

That image brings it all together. For, in those first generations of the Church, the most common phrase used to describe the Eucharist was "the sacrifice." Both the *Didache* (a document of the mid-first century) and St. Ignatius refer to it as "*the* sacrifice." And yet martyrdom, too, was "*the sacrifice*."

God's Wheat, Ground

And so, in A.D. 107, when Ignatius described his own impending execution, he used eucharistic terms. He said he was like the wine at the offertory. He wrote to the Romans, "Grant me nothing more than that I be poured out to God, while an altar is still ready." Later in the same letter he wrote: "Let me be food for the wild beasts, through whom I can reach God. I am God's wheat, ground fine by the lion's teeth to be made purest bread for Christ."[5] Ignatius was bread and he was wine; his martyrdom was a sacrifice. It was, in a sense, a eucharist.

Ignatius's good friend St. Polycarp also died a martyr's death. Polycarp was bishop of Smyrna, and had been converted by the apostle John. His secretary described the bishop's martyrdom, once again, as a kind of eucharist. Polycarp's final words are a long prayer of thanksgiving that echoes the great eucharistic prayers of the ancient world and today. It includes an invocation of the Holy Spirit, a doxology of the Trinity, and a great Amen at the end.

When the flames reached the body of the old bishop, his secretary tells us that the pyre gave off not the odor of burning flesh but the aroma of baking bread.[6] In yet another martyrdom, then, we find a pure offering of bread—again, a eucharist.

The eucharistic images in Ignatius and Polycarp echo again in the future writings and histories of the martyrs. Even in the court transcripts, presumably taken down by pagan Romans, the Christians reply to the charges against them with lines from the liturgy, lifting up their hearts to God. And when they are sentenced, they say *Deo gratias*—"thanks be to God."

The story of the martyr Pionius is told, verbatim, in the words of the eucharistic prayer: "and looking up to heaven he gave thanks to God."[7] The Greek word for "thanks" is *eucharistesas*. So we might read it as, "Looking up to heaven, he offered the Eucharist to God," even as the flames consumed him. In a similar way, the priest Irenaeus cried out, in the midst of torture, "With my endurance I am even now offering sacrifice to my God to whom I have always offered sacrifice."[8]

So pervasive is this eucharistic language in the early Church's account of martyrdom that one of the great scholars of Christian antiquity, Robin Darling Young of the University of Notre Dame, has spoken of the ancient Church as having two liturgies: the private liturgy of the Eucharist and the public liturgy of martyrdom.[9]

LOVING EUCHARIST

But what is it about martyrdom that makes it like the Eucharist? Well, what has Jesus done in the Eucharist? He has given himself to us, and he has held nothing back. He gives us his body, blood, soul, and divinity. He gives himself to us as food. And that is love: the total gift of self. That is the very love the martyrs wanted to emulate. Jesus had given himself entirely for them. They wanted to give themselves entirely for him—everything they had, holding nothing back. If Jesus would become bread for them, they would allow the lions to make them finest wheat for Jesus.

So, martyrdom was a total gift of self; the Eucharist was a total gift of self. In the Eucharist, Jesus gave himself to Christians. In martyrdom, Christians gave themselves back to him.

But there's a problem here. Very few of the ancient Christians died for the faith. What about the rest? What was their gift? How did they live the Eucharist?

Not long after Christianity was legalized in A.D. 312, St. Jerome noted that some believers were already growing nostalgic for the good old days of the martyrs. But Jerome put a halt to such fantasies. He told his congregation, "Let's not think that there is martyrdom only in the shedding of blood. There is *always* martyrdom." [10]

There is always martyrdom. For most of the early Christians, the martyrdom came not with lions or fire or the rack or the sword. It came not at the hands of a mob or a gladiator. For most of the early Christians, "martyrdom" consisted in a daily dying to self in imitation of Jesus Christ.

Jesus told them, "If any want to become my followers, let them deny themselves . . . daily" (Luke 9:23). So the Christians denied themselves, in imitation of Jesus. What did this mean, in practical terms? It meant that they would never eat lavishly as long as others were going hungry. They would never keep an opulent wardrobe while others dressed in rags. They would never hold back their testimony to the faith as long as *any* of their neighbors were living in sin or in ignorance of the love of Jesus Christ. In the early years of the third century in North Africa, Tertullian noted that even the pagans were impressed by the Christians' selfless giving: "It is our care of the helpless, our practice of loving kindness that brands us in the eyes of many of our opponents, who say, 'See those Christians, how they love one another.'"[11]

There was *always* martyrdom, even though the martyrs who were thrown to the lions or crucified or beheaded were very few in number. Countless others gave witness through the giving of themselves, until they had nothing left to give. St. Paul had, long before, addressed this in his Letter to the Romans, where he wrote: "I appeal to you therefore, brothers and sisters, by the mercies of God, to present your bodies as a living sacrifice, holy and acceptable to God, which is your spiritual worship" (Romans 12:1).

NERO'S WORK OF EVANGELIZATION

In the midst of Nero's horrors, Peter and Paul both came to Rome—Paul in chains, Peter willingly. Eusebius tells us that they both died on the same day.[12]

Peter was crucified. This time, he didn't deny Jesus or try to run away. He made only one request: he asked his executioners to crucify him upside down. He said he wasn't worthy to die the same way as his Lord.

Paul, who was a Roman citizen, couldn't be crucified—that was one of the privileges of being a citizen. Instead, he was beheaded—a quick, neat death compared to the slow agony of crucifixion.

Nero's persecution established a legal precedent for the persecutions to come. From then on, Christianity was a more or less illegal cult, and the punishment for it was death. Rome's enforcement, however, waxed and waned in severity over the next 260 years. Especially bloody persecutions happened during the reigns of Domitian (81–95), Trajan (98–117), Antoninus Pius (138–61), Marcus Aurelius (161–80), Septimius Severus (193–211), Decius (249–51), Valerian (253–60), Diocletian (284–305), and Galerius (305–11). Even between persecutions, however, Christians were never quite safe. Government personnel could change at any moment with the death or promotion of a governor, and mob violence, which often went unpunished, could erupt at any time.

Still, the extreme cruelty of Nero's Christian "spectacles" served a useful and providential purpose. It made the Christians much more visible, and it made them objects of sympathy, at least to some Romans. By creating so many martyrs, Nero may well have been responsible for thousands of conversions. History would repeatedly prove the truth of Tertullian's maxim: "The blood of the martyrs is seed"[13]—the seed of the Church. ❧

A Closer Look . . .

The Popes and Rome

In the Acts of the Apostles, we see the center of Christian activity shift from Jerusalem to Rome. The capital of the Roman Empire was the ultimate earthly destination of the two great apostles, Peter and Paul.

Ancient traditions are unanimous in recording that both Peter and Paul were martyred in Rome. The earliest Christians made pilgrimages to the apostles' tombs there and left pious graffiti along the way. Visitors to Rome can still view these scrawled messages today.

Simon Peter had received authority when Jesus pronounced him the "rock" on whom he would build his Church (Matthew 16:18). In the years after Pentecost, Peter served as the spokesman, judge, teacher, preacher, and healer in the community. This authority remained with him until his death, and it transferred to the men who succeeded him as bishop of Rome.

Before the end of the first century, Pope St. Clement of Rome wrote fatherly letters to reprove and instruct the Christians in distant Corinth. The letters were read in the liturgy at Corinth for centuries.

Less than ten years later, St. Ignatius, who succeeded Peter as bishop of Antioch, wrote letters of instruction to many churches, but deferred only to one Church: the Church of Rome.

At the end of the second century, St. Irenaeus confirmed the primacy of Rome and the papacy. The bishop of Lyons cited "that tradition derived from the Apostles, of the very great, the very ancient, and universally known Church founded and organized at Rome by the two most glorious Apostles, Peter and Paul . . . which comes down to our time by means of the successions of the bishops. For it is a matter of necessity that every Church should agree with this Church, on account of its preeminent authority—that is, the faithful everywhere inasmuch as the apostolic tradition has been preserved continuously by faithful men everywhere."[14] Irenaeus also supplied a complete list of popes, from Peter to his own day.

Throughout the era of the Church Fathers, many great saints appealed to the pope for help and for judgment: St. Athanasius, St. Basil of Caesarea, St. Jerome, St. John Chrysostom, St. Augustine, and St. Cyril of Alexandria, among others. Theodoret of Cyr put the matter eloquently: "If Paul, the herald of the Truth, the trumpet of the Holy Ghost, had recourse to the great Peter, in order to obtain a decision from him for those at Antioch who were disputing about living by the Law, much more do we small and humble folk run to the Apostolic See to get healing from you for the sores of the churches. For it is fitting that you should in all things have the pre-eminence, seeing that your See possesses many peculiar privileges."[15]

Sts. Peter and Paul have always shared a single feast day. On that feast day in 441, Pope St. Leo the Great preached a homily rejoicing that he could trace his own lineage in an unbroken line to the greatest of the apostles. Modern popes can make the same claim.

"These are the men," said Leo, "through whom the light of Christ's gospel shone on you, O Rome, and through whom you, who were the teacher of error, were made the disciple of Truth. These are your holy Fathers and true shepherds, who gave you claim to be numbered among the heavenly kingdoms. . . . They promoted you to such glory . . . the head of the world through St. Peter's Holy See."[16]

Mary and the Early Church

The Church's first expressions of Marian devotion were beautiful and memorable. They have been passed intact from generation to generation, and are still used today. Mary is in the early creeds and in St. Ignatius of Antioch's professions of faith. In the middle of the second century, St. Justin described her as the "New Eve."[17] Like the first Eve, Mary was mother of all the living—now those who are alive in Christ. The earliest recorded Marian prayer was in use in Egypt in the third century (and possibly earlier). Catholics still pray that prayer today: "We fly to your patronage, O holy Mother of God. Despise not our petitions in our need, and keep us from all danger. O ever glorious and faithful Virgin Mary!" The oldest surviving images of Mary are in the catacombs, the early Christian burial chambers, in Rome. Those paintings show her holding the infant Jesus in her arms. The earliest known report of a Marian apparition also comes from the third century, when she appeared to St. Gregory the Wonderworker.

2

The Case for Christianity

It was difficult for outsiders to understand the early Christians. They prayed for the emperor, but unlike other patriotic citizens, they refused to offer sacrifices to his guardian spirit, his "genius." They loved everyone, even as they taught that everyone was a sinner (thus earning Nero's charge of "hatred of humanity"). Rejected by pious Jews, they claimed to be heirs to a spiritual Israel.

So the early believers were misunderstood by both pagans [Non-Christians] and Jews. Wild rumors flew about the Christians' secret ceremonies. Both pagans and Jews charged them with cannibalism, infanticide, and (of course) disloyalty to the emperor. We've just seen how Nero found the Christians a convenient target when someone had to be blamed for the fire in Rome. If people believed that the Christians were cannibals, it was easy to believe that they were arsonists, too.

But at the beginning of the second century, a movement of Christian teachers spoke up to set the record straight. These teachers are known as the "apologists." Perhaps the greatest of their first generation was St. Justin, who was born about the year 100.

The apologists set out to give reasoned explanations of Christian doctrines. (An "apology" in this sense is not the admission of a fault, but speech or writing that defends some idea.) They were not so much preachers as debaters. Amid a hostile and confused culture, they methodically explained and defended all that Christians *really* believed.

Justin was well prepared for this task. As a young man, a pagan of Samaria, he was an intense seeker looking for wisdom in all the usual places in the ancient world. He studied philosophy, rhetoric, history, and poetry. He pushed his inquiries to ultimate questions, to first principles, but no master in any of the philosophy schools was able to satisfy him. (Justin abandoned one philosopher who demanded cash in advance from his disciples.)

One day Justin was walking along a beach, where he met an old man. Soon the two were deep in a discussion of the ultimate questions. Justin identified himself as a philosopher.

"Does philosophy, then, make happiness?" asked the old man.

"Surely," said Justin, "and only philosophy."

"What, then, is philosophy?" the man asked. "And what is happiness?"

"Philosophy," replied Justin, "is the knowledge of what really exists, and a clear perception of the truth; and happiness is the reward of such knowledge and wisdom."

"But what do you call God?" said the old man.

From there, the old man led Justin to see that, if he sincerely sought truth and the God who really exists, he needed to consult the prophets of ancient Israel. "They alone," said the mysterious stranger, "both saw and announced the truth . . . not influenced by a desire for glory, but filled with the Holy Spirit. Their writings still exist, and whoever reads them gains much in his knowledge of . . . all a philosopher ought to know."[1]

Justin went off at once to find these books, and on reading he found much more: "Immediately a flame was kindled in my soul; and I was possessed by a love of the prophets, and of those who are friends of Christ. . . . I found this philosophy alone to be safe and profitable."[2] Tradition says he was baptized in Ephesus.

Studying Christian doctrine, Justin discovered that much of what he had learned about Christianity from the pagans was utterly false. He was further distressed that these rumor campaigns were leading to the persecution of Christians. So he dedicated himself to the refutation of these errors, explaining and defending his adopted faith before pagans and Jews. Two of his "apologies" are addressed to the emperor Antoninus Pius and the Roman Senate.

Justin still identified himself as a philosopher, and he still wore the traditional philosopher's cloak. He saw everything that was good and true in pagan philosophy as a glimpse of the truth and goodness of God revealed in Jesus Christ.

Justin's *First Apology* gives us one of the clearest descriptions we have of what the Mass was like in the early and middle 100s—roughly a century after Christ's resurrection—and it is a description that looks very familiar:

On the day called Sunday, all who live in cities or in the country gather together to one place, and the memoirs of the apostles or the writings of the prophets are read, as long as time permits; then, when the reader has ceased, the president verbally instructs, and exhorts to the imitation of these good things. Then we all rise together and pray, and, as we said before, when our prayer is ended, bread and wine and water are brought, and the president in like manner offers prayers and thanksgivings, according to his ability, and the people assent, saying Amen; and there is a distribution to each, and a participation of that over which thanks have been given, and to those who are absent a portion is sent by the deacons. And they who are well to do, and willing, give what each thinks fit; and what is collected is deposited with the president, who succors the orphans and widows and those who, through sickness or any other cause, are in want, and those who are in bonds and the strangers sojourning among us, and in a word takes care of all who are in need.

But Sunday is the day on which we all hold our common assembly, because it is the first day on which God, having wrought a change in the darkness and matter, made the world; and Jesus Christ our Savior on the same day rose from the dead. For he was crucified on the day before Saturday; and on the day after Saturday, which is the day of the Sun, having appeared to his apostles and disciples, he taught them these things, which we have submitted to you also for your consideration.[3]

Already we can see that Sunday celebrations resembled our liturgy today. The congregation heard readings from the gospels and the prophets, and then there was a sermon. They celebrated the Eucharist, and there was an offering for the poor. A modern Catholic suddenly transported back through time to the year 150 or so would recognize what was going on in church on Sunday.

Eventually Justin traveled to Rome, where he established a school of Christian philosophy. However, a Christian couldn't make such a public spectacle of himself and get away with it. Consequently, in about the year 165, Justin was charged with impiety toward the gods and, with six companions, was scourged and beheaded. Thus he earned the title by which the Church has always known him: St. Justin Martyr.

WHEN LIFE WAS ROTTEN

As philosophers, men like Justin persuaded at least some of the empire's cultural elites to give Christianity a fair hearing. But philosophy alone cannot account for the groundswell of conversions in those early centuries. Remember: the Church grew, for two and a half centuries, at a fairly steady rate of 40 percent per decade.

Why were the Christians so successful? Mainly it was because Christianity made a real difference in people's lives.

Especially in the cities, where the Christian religion took hold first, life could be rotten for ordinary people. Most lived in cramped, smoky tenements with no ventilation or plumbing. Life expectancy was around thirty years for men, and perhaps much lower for women. Hygiene was minimal. Medical care was more dangerous than disease, and disease often left its victims disfigured or dead. The human body was host to countless parasites, and tenements were infested by rats and other pests. For entertainment, people thronged the circuses to see other people mutilated and killed. The corpses of those who died of natural causes were sometimes left to rot in open sewers. It was a miserable life for many people.

And pagan marriage offered no respite from this misery. Greco-Roman women were usually married at age eleven or twelve, to a mate who was not of their choosing. Afterward, many suffered in predatory relationships rife with abortion and adultery. Infanticide was common, especially for female or defective offspring. Of the six hundred families who show up in the records from ancient Delphi, only six had raised more than one daughter. Although most of those six hundred families were quite large, they had all routinely killed their baby girls. And this was not a geographically isolated trend. A recent archaeological dig in the Near East turned up an ancient sewer clogged with the bones of newborns—hundreds of newborns—presumably all of them female.[4]

If few girls lived to see the day after their birth, still more died on their way to adulthood. The shortage of women, then, played further havoc on the population growth of the empire, as well as on its economy and its morals.

The Christian Difference

That's the world into which the early Christians were born, the world where they grew up and married, and where they raised their families. It was a world characterized by a culture of death.

But Christian marriage and child rearing immediately set believers apart from the prevailing culture. Christian husbands and wives genuinely tried to love one another, as their religion required. Their mutual affection and their openness to bearing children led to a higher birth rate, and thus to a still higher growth rate for the early Church.

The early Christians' respect for the dignity of marriage made the faith enormously attractive to pagan women. Thus, women made up a disproportionate number of the early converts. This situation, in turn, made Christianity enormously attractive to pagan men—who couldn't find many pagan women to marry, but saw young ladies attending the Christian liturgy in great numbers.

Christian faith, then as now, makes for happy homes. And, in pagan cultures, then as now, happy homes were very attractive. The evidence seems to indicate that, in the ancient Roman Empire, Christian homes were the Church's primary place of evangelization. = writing abt christ Mom s = Evangelization

Epidemics were among the great terrors of life in the ancient world. The physicians in those days knew that diseases were communicable, but they knew nothing about bacteria or viruses, never mind antibiotics or antisepsis. So, once a contagious disease hit a city or town, there was really no stopping it. There were several major epidemics during the rise of Christianity, and each of them reduced the empire's population by about one-third.

Plague

Yet even in these circumstances, the Church grew. In fact, amid simultaneous persecutions and epidemics, the Church grew still more dramatically, especially in proportion to the total population of the empire.

left for 2-3 weeks

How did the Church manage to grow while masses of people were dying from disease? Look at what ordinarily occurred when an epidemic hit a region or city. The first people to leave were the doctors. They knew what was coming, and they knew they could do little to prevent it.

The next to leave were the pagan priests, because they had the means and the freedom to do so.

Ordinary pagan families were encouraged to abandon their homes when family members contracted the plague. Again, they knew no other way to isolate the disease than to leave the afflicted family member behind to die, perhaps slowly, perhaps quickly.

Christians stayed

Yet Christians were duty-bound not to abandon the sick. Jesus had said that, in caring for the sick, Christians were caring for him (see Mathew 25:39-40). So, even though Christians knew no more about medicine than the pagans did, they stayed with their family members, friends, and neighbors who were suffering.

Consider this account of the great epidemic of the year 260, left to us by Bishop Dionysius of Alexandria:

> Most of our brother Christians showed unbounded love and loyalty, never sparing themselves and thinking only of one another. Heedless of danger, they took charge of the sick, attending their every need and ministering to them in Christ—and with them departed this life serenely happy; for they were infected by others with the disease, drawing on themselves the sickness of their neighbors and cheerfully accepting their pains. . . . Death in this form, the result of great piety and strong faith, seems in every way the equal of martyrdom.[5]

willing to die happily

We also possess pagan accounts of that epidemic, and all of them are characterized by despair. Yet the Christians were "serenely happy." Amid all that havoc, Christian charity, which usually began in the family home, had an enormous impact on Church growth. Christians were much more likely to survive epidemics because they cared for one another. Mere comfort care cut the mortality rate of the Christians by two-thirds when compared to that of the pagans.

Pagans became christian

What's more, the Christian families cared for their pagan neighbors. The pagans who received Christian care were more likely to survive and, in turn, become Christians themselves. Thus, in times of epidemic, when the population as a whole plummeted, Church growth soared.

And the pagans took notice. The emperor Julian, who despised Christianity and led the charge to bring paganism back to the empire, had to admire Christian charity, at least grudgingly:

"The impious Galileans support not only their poor, but ours as well. Everyone can see that our poor lack aid from us."[6]

There were obvious advantages to Christianity—and obvious disadvantages to paganism. The pagan religion, for example, was linked to the Roman government. Pagans were expected to worship the emperor, or at least his "genius," as a god. But for the next few decades, even as the Christian Church grew and prospered, the pagan empire was torn apart by one civil war after another. Marauding armies devastated whole provinces. And the cause of all these wars was always the same: too many emperors. How could anyone seriously entertain the idea of emperor as god when sometimes six or more emperor-gods were battering each other and anyone who got in their way?

In the West, it eventually came down to Constantine and Maxentius, and popular feeling was on Constantine's side. Maxentius was a cruel tyrant, and probably insane as well. But Maxentius held Rome and the Italian peninsula. Italy prepared for another of those destructive but ultimately meaningless battles between rival emperors that litter the history of the empire. However, this time something different happened. On the eve of the battle, Constantine made a decision that changed the empire forever.

THE VISION THAT CHANGED THE WORLD

On October 28, 312, the battle lines were drawn, when suddenly Constantine had a vision. Eusebius, who heard it from the lips of Constantine himself, tells it this way:

About midday, when the sun was beginning to decline, he saw with his own eyes the trophy of a cross of light in the heavens, above the sun, and bearing the inscription CON-QUER BY THIS. He himself was struck with amazement, and his whole army also.[7]

Under the sign of the cross, Constantine won the battle. Not surprisingly, as soon as he was established as Augustus, the Roman title used for the emperor, he began to show special favor to the Christians. He immediately ordered that a statue of himself with the cross be erected in the center of Rome, where everyone would see it, and this inscription was written under it in large letters: "By this saving sign, the true proof of courage, I saved your city from the yoke of the tyrant and set her free; furthermore I freed the Senate and People of Rome and restored them to their ancient renown and splendor."[8]

At the time, the emperor Licinius controlled most of the eastern half of the empire. When Constantine met Licinius in Milan in 313, the two issued an edict proclaiming freedom of religion for everyone. For the first time in human history, absolute freedom of religion was the official policy of a great world power. The Edict of Milan was something truly new in the world, and it was really Constantine's idea—Licinius just went along with it because it seemed best to do what Constantine said.

The drunken pagan Maximin still ruled part of the East, but he so was afraid of the combined power of Constantine and Licinius that he grudgingly accepted the decree. It wasn't long before Licinius eliminated Maximin. When Licinius began persecuting the Christians in the East in 320, Constantine in turn eliminated him. By 324 Constantine was sole emperor of the whole Roman Empire, and the Christian Church was free to come out into the open everywhere. The Church, the friend of

freedom of religion [handwritten marginal note]

the poor and despised, was suddenly rich and respected.

It is important for us to recognize Constantine's role in Christian history. The Church Fathers gave him credit for bringing about the "peace of the Church," but we shouldn't overemphasize the value of his role, because Constantine didn't so much ensure Christianity's success as acknowledge it. His edict of toleration was overdue recognition that the Church had already won the empire. Christians, in fact, were already in the majority. The real credit should go largely to the quiet, private witness of Christian families, the powerful persuasions of apologists like Justin, and the heroic public witness of the martyrs. 🐚

A Closer Look . . .

The Value of Virginity

"Consecrated virgins" were those Christians, especially women, who chose to live celibate lives of prayer, work, intensive study, and service, all the while remaining "in the world." Most, it seems, continued to live in their family homes. The homilies, tracts, and legislation of the early Church Fathers discuss consecrated virgins about as often as they mention the clergy.

The way Christians esteemed virgins was revolutionary in its time, and it spoke volumes about the greater rights women would win through Christianity's triumph. The Church viewed these women as prophets, teachers, role models, and leaders. In the fourth century, St. Jerome wrote, in his letter of praise for the Roman virgin Asella, that priests and bishops "should look up to her." In the liturgy in the third century, consecrated virgins were given a place of honor, receiving Communion before the rest of the laity.

Perhaps the modern Christian cannot fully appreciate how revolutionary this was—not only for women to be so esteemed, but for *unmarried* women to be esteemed at all.

In ancient cultures, a woman's value was almost exclusively derived from the males with whom she was in relation: her husband, her sons, or her father. If a woman never married (and so never bore sons), she was almost certainly destined to poverty and obscurity. In Israel, where marriage was considered a duty and barrenness or infertility was considered a curse or punishment for sin, there was no place or esteem for an unmarried woman.

Yet Christianity—with its cult of two prominent virgins, Jesus and Mary—turned that value system upside down. This is evident in Scripture, in the Acts of the Apostles (see, for example, 21:9) as well as in St. Paul's lengthy treatment of consecrated virginity in his First Letter to the Corinthians (see all of chapter 7).

Now, the consecrated single or celibate life was honored, and virgins (and widows) were seen as deserving the direct support of the Christian community.

3

Heresy and Orthodoxy

Even before Christianity was legal, there had been divisions in the Church. Doctrines about crucial issues like the Trinity and the divinity of Christ were still in development or not written down, and debate often raged about these and other topics. Periodically, ideas contrary to orthodox Christianity gained popularity, and then a "heresy"—from the Greek word for "faction" or "choice"—would spread.

Of all the ancient heresies, Arianism gained the strongest following and most attention. Its central idea was that the Son of God was not equal to the Father—not divine, but a perfect creature. Starting in Alexandria, the heresy spread rapidly, winning over, at different times, several eastern emperors, a majority of the bishops, and most of the Christians in the Germanic tribes. Arian missionaries had been very active among the barbarians, and many of the tribes surrounding the empire had embraced Arian Christianity. The doctrine spread so quickly, St. Jerome quipped, that it seemed as if one day "the world woke up to find itself Arian."[1] When St. Athanasius took up the opposition to Arianism, he drew upon himself the motto "Athanasius against the world."

AMBROSE: FROM CATECHUMEN TO BISHOP

In 374, the Arian bishop of Milan died. At that time, Milan was the largest city in the West, surpassing Rome itself, and it was divided between Catholics and Arians. Catholics in the city wanted an orthodox bishop, and the Arians, of course, wanted an Arian. There were threats of riots at the cathedral. Ambrose, the local governor, who had a reputation for scrupulous honesty and fairness, went out into the streets to calm the people. Suddenly a cry went up from the crowd: "Ambrose for bishop!"

Arians and Catholics agreed: the beloved governor Ambrose should be the next bishop. The only problem was that he was still a catechumen, studying in preparation for his baptism but as of yet not baptized.

That didn't stop the people of Milan. At first Ambrose tried to refuse the honor. But when Emperor Valentinian confirmed his appointment, he reluctantly accepted. Ambrose was baptized and ordained almost at the same time—and then he returned to his catechism tutor for some intense studying. He gave away his considerable fortune, retaining only enough to support his sister, a nun.

Ambrose turned out to be a superb and completely orthodox bishop. His political experience gave him the knowledge he needed to work with the decaying Roman government, and his simple charity won the hearts of everyone he met.

Ambrose developed a distinctive way of dealing with secular authority. In the East, the fourth-century historian Eusebius, who exalted the emperor Constantine, had set forth the view that the Christian king was God's instrument for bringing about heaven's kingdom on earth.

Ambrose, on the other hand, made a stricter distinction between what was Caesar's and what was God's. He insisted that only the Church could decide on sacred matters, which became the model for distinguishing sacred and secular authority in the West.

There were many opportunities for Ambrose to put this concept into practice. When the Arian mother of Emperor Valentinian moved to Milan, she asked her son to give her control of several churches. Valentinian agreed. Ambrose incited the people to occupy the churches, singing hymns, until the emperor backed down. Ambrose won: the emperor wasn't willing to start a violent riot. When Valentinian tried to summon a council of the Church, as Constantine had done decades earlier, Ambrose declined to attend. And when Theodosius the Great, furious at an insurrection in Thessalonica, ordered that seven thousand of the inhabitants of the city be killed, Ambrose excommunicated him until he did public penance for his sin.

St. Augustine Makes a Ladder of His Vices

In 383, Ambrose met a young, brilliant, and somewhat brash schoolteacher from Africa whose name was Augustine. The two became friends. It was a friendship that would change history.

Augustine was born in Tagaste, North Africa, the son of a pagan Roman official and a Christian mother. His mother, Monica, raised him in the Christian faith. But at the age of sixteen, Augustine left for the city of Carthage to study law, and then literature and philosophy. In Carthage, he encountered a host of temptations and gradually gave up his faith. At age seventeen, he took a mistress, who in 372 bore him a son, Adeodatus. Augustine would live with this woman for the next seventeen years, but he never married her.

Augustine had a voracious mind, eager to know everything. Having lost his faith in God, he took to reflecting on the material world. Especially troubling to him was the problem of evil. He was attracted by the doctrines of a sect called the Manicheans, which seemed to explain the material world and the problem of evil. Matter was evil, the Manicheans believed, because it was fashioned by an evil creator. Augustine was never quite convinced of the teachings of the sect, but for the next ten years he associated with its adherents. His beloved Christian mother prayed constantly for his conversion.

Meanwhile, Augustine was building a solid reputation as a teacher of rhetoric. In 383, he moved to Rome, but a few months later, he went to Milan to make more money and met Ambrose.

Bishop Ambrose had the same eager mind as Augustine. But he had something else, too—a sense of peace, which attracted the young teacher, Augustine. The elder man was patient, and gave Augustine his precious time in long conversation.

Augustine returned to the faith of his childhood in 387, and he began to live in a contemplative community with his mother, his brother, his son, and some friends. "Our hearts are restless, O Lord, until they rest in You," he would one day write.[2] His heart had found rest, though he would again know sadness. His mother died later in 387; his son died in 389. *Everyone died*

Augustine returned to North Africa, where the Christians of Hippo pressed him to receive holy orders. In 395, he was ordained a bishop.

Augustine wrote an astounding number of books in the years that followed, even as he kept a demanding pastoral schedule— preaching, teaching candidates for baptism, answering correspondence from throughout the world, and daily receiving the complaints and petitions of local believers.

Having once studied heresy himself, Bishop Augustine found

shrewd and successful ways of counteracting the sects and healing the schisms in the lands under his authority. Historians credit him for dealing mortal blows to three major heresies: Manicheanism, Donatism, and Pelagianism. He also welcomed back the Tertullianists and Montanists who had gone into schism centuries before. Augustine's primary weapons against heresy were charity and truth.

CYRIL THE VIRILE

Augustine had his methods and his gifts. Other saints had other methods and other gifts, and they dealt with heresies as God led them. Augustine's contemporary, St. Cyril of Alexandria, is a case in point.

Cyril of Alexandria was the nephew of Theophilus, his predecessor as patriarch archbishop of Alexandria in Egypt. Cyril likely spent his youth in a monastery before his uncle drafted him as an assistant and secretary. In 402, he accompanied Theophilus to the notorious Synod of the Oak that deposed John Chrysostom, sending the saint to his exile and death. Theophilus was among John's accusers and persecutors, and it seems likely that Cyril shared his opinions (although later in life he would show signs of a change of heart).

Theophilus died in 412, and Cyril succeeded him—but only after a riot between his supporters and those of his rival. From the start, Cyril treated heretics and schismatics rather severely, which won him enduring opposition. Cyril also had the ill fortune to live in a time when relations between Christians and Jews in Egypt had escalated to open street violence. The Christians received little support from the governor, so Cyril assembled a rough and undisciplined guard of his own, with some truly awful results.

No one disputes that Cyril was an irascible character and something of a political operator. Yet he was also a man of crystalline intellect and tremendous courage, defending the truth, no matter what the cost. He was unwilling to compromise doctrine, even if it placed him in opposition to the Christian emperor. And Cyril was always willing to suffer the consequences: he was imprisoned for defending the doctrine that defined the Blessed Virgin Mary as the Mother of God. Cyril was, moreover, a brilliant dogmatic theologian. He is best known for opposing the teaching of Nestorius, a monk from Antioch who became patriarch of Constantinople. Nestorius opposed the use of the Greek term *Theotokos* ("God-bearer" or "Mother of God") to describe Mary. He preferred *Christotokos*, or "Christ-bearer," arguing that Mary could not be God's mother because she was not his origin but was rather the mother of Jesus' human nature. Cyril argued, to the contrary, that a mother does not give birth to a nature, but to a person. To deny the title to Mary, then, was to divide Jesus Christ into two subjects, two persons, two "I's."

Matters came to a head at the Council of Ephesus in 431, where Cyril's arguments won the day. Despite the oppressive summer heat—which killed several of the bishops at council—an enormous crowd of ordinary Christians had assembled at Ephesus. And when, at night, they heard the news of the bishops' decision, they let out a raucous shout and carried the council fathers through the streets of the city in a torchlight procession, singing Marian hymns with great gusto.

Still, once the bishops returned home, many were reluctant to enforce the decrees of the council. Nestorius tried to summon countercouncils. And Cyril was even, for a brief time, deposed from the patriarchate. Once the dust settled on the controversies, he resumed his voluminous correspondence and work on his Scripture commentary. St. Cyril died in 444, after an episcopate of nearly thirty-two years.

The Rise of Islam

Cyril lived in a time of increasing disorder, not only in doctrinal matters but also in civil government. Augustine had died while the Vandals were attacking Hippo. The Roman Empire was collapsing all around Cyril. Soon there would be nothing left of the empire in the West. The eastern half, with its capital at Constantinople, was still intact, but that, too, was about to face its greatest challenge.

In the year 610, an Arab merchant named Mohammed announced that he had received a vision from God (*Allah* in Arabic). Allah had asked him to bring to the world a message that was written in a book called the Koran, translated as "the reading." At first, Mohammed had little success, but soon his movement grew. Mohammed the prophet also became a military leader, and in 630, captured Mecca. The new religion spread as quickly as Christianity had, but with a big difference. Whereas Christianity had spread by persuasion, Islam was spreading by force. Christ had allowed his enemies to kill him; the prophet Mohammed, armed with a sword, wasn't about to take that chance.

Under Mohammed's successors, the Muslim conquests rapidly mounted. Within ten years of the prophet's death, the Muslims had conquered nearly the entire eastern and southern areas of the Roman Empire. Jerusalem, Alexandria, and all of Egypt and Syria had fallen, and the Arabs were threatening Constantinople itself. Soon the rest of North Africa was theirs, and then Spain. There the expansion finally stopped, halted by the heroic resistance of the West Germanic tribes called the Franks, under Charles Martel.

Why did the Christian empire fall apart so quickly? Partly it was because of the enthusiasm of the Muslim soldiers and the talent of their leaders. But a greater reason was that the people were disillusioned with the leaders of Constantinople. Rigid enforcement of orthodoxy—accompanied by pillage and massacre in heretical towns—had left gaping wounds in just those places where the Muslims conquered most easily. The Christian heretics who had been persecuted by the empire would be tolerated by the Arabs. And many of them would find Islam itself attractive, because Islam maintained several familiar details of the Christian religion.

For example, Muslims believe that Jesus was the Messiah, miraculously born of the Virgin Mary. But they do not consider him to be God or the Son of God. According to Islamic belief, the "People of the Book"—Christians and Jews—had received the truth from Allah, the one God, but they had corrupted it. There is only one God, and the one God could not possibly have a son.

To a faithful Muslim, Islam did not begin with Mohammed; it began with Adam. Abraham, Jacob, Jesus, and all the biblical prophets were faithful Muslims. So it was necessary for God to send another prophet, Mohammed, to sort out the confusion created by the Christians and the Jews.

Some of the later Fathers of the Church considered Islam a Christian heresy. In fact, Islam was strikingly similar to the other Christian heresies that had been popular all over the East. The Arians also had denied the divinity of Christ; they would agree with the Koran that Jesus is not to be worshipped as God. The Nestorians denied Mary the title Mother of God. And the Montanists believed that God continued to send new revelations through new prophets. All these people had suffered dreadful persecutions under the Christian emperor Justinian and his successors. Was it any wonder that many of them welcomed the Islamic Arabs as liberators? And was it any wonder that many of them found Islam easy to accept?

Nevertheless, the conquered countries didn't turn Islamic all at once. Many Christians—probably a majority at first—remained faithful, and even now there are significant Christian minorities in most of those Islamic countries. But the Muslim conquerors put policies in place to ensure that Islam would gradually win out. It's true that they tolerated the Christians and the Jews, but they tolerated them as obvious inferiors. Christians could continue to worship, but they couldn't build new churches or rebuild old ones that fell apart. They had to pay double taxes, so there was a strong financial incentive to convert. They couldn't try to convert Muslims. In many places, Christians had to wear distinctive clothes. In short, to be a Christian was to live with daily persecution, even if the persecution was milder than that of Justinian against the heretics. On the other hand, to convert to Islam brought instant advantages.

Taking a long-range view, the Muslim conquerors were mostly content to let Christianity wither away rather than try to eliminate it all at once. After a while, Christianity—once the dominant religion in northern Africa, southern Europe, and western Asia—would become mostly a European religion, and it would remain that way for hundreds of years.

But that did not mean Christianity was dead in the East.

With the Nestorian schism in the fifth century, many disaffected Christians took refuge in the Persian East, which was beyond the political influence of Constantinople. For hundreds of years, the East Syrians went their way, having little contact with the West, but sending missions to China and India. Through the centuries, some of these churches returned to communion with the West, though others kept communion with the churches descended from Nestorius, the fifth-century theologian who had gone astray. After more than a millennium of separation, the gap between the Nestorians and the West might seem unbridgeable. But hope is a virtue always in season. "For a thousand years in your sight are like yesterday when it is past" (Psalm 90:4).

In 1994, Pope John Paul II signed a Common Christological Declaration with Patriarch Mar Dinkha IV, essentially resolving "the main dogmatic problem between the Catholic Church and the Assyrian Church"—in other words, clearing up the Nestorian troubles once and for all. In 2001, the Pontifical Council for Promoting Christian Unity went a step further and approved the sharing of Communion between the (Catholic) Chaldean Church and the (so-called Nestorian) Assyrian Church of the East. Christians who had kept faith through fourteen centuries of disdain and persecution were at last in communion with the Catholic Church.

God gathered the scattered. That is one way the early Christians understood Christ's redemption: as the recovery of many lost sheep and the convergence of all flocks into one fold with one shepherd, a divine shepherd who is always faithful. Thus, when heresies and schisms divide the Church, God calls forth pastors like Ambrose and theologians like Augustine. And sometimes, when words fail, he lets time heal wounds. ༄

A Closer Look . . .

The Mother Church of the East

Known as "the Mother Church" by Byzantine Christians, the Church of Hagia Sophia ("Holy Wisdom"), stood for nine hundred years as the center of the Empire and of eastern Christianity.

The emperor Justinian knew he was building a church for all time. He nearly bankrupted Constantinople to build it. The city watched one fountain after another dry up–all the pipes had been melted down to make gutters for the new church. The teachers in the schools were starving. The poor were poorer, and the rich complained of being somewhat less rich. But the church was going up, and for a while Justinian hardly seemed to care about anything else.

His architect, Anthemius, was a brilliant but slightly eccentric engineer. Anthemius invented a kind of searchlight, and he used it to play practical jokes on his neighbors. He also invented a steam engine, but it was only a mechanical toy. Anthemius was just the sort of mildly unbalanced architect who would try something just because it was supposed to be impossible, and just the sort to build the most magnificent church in the world–or die trying.

The impossible problem was this: how do you give a building both light and space? The bigger the building, the heavier the roof. The heavier the roof, the thicker the supports it needs, and the less space there is for letting in light.

Anthemius' answer was a huge, shallow dome. It ought to have been impossible. Nothing like it had ever been done before—a big dome usually has to be tall, like the dome of St. Peter's in Rome or the Capitol building in Washington, in order to hold itself up. Even if the dome could be built, the supports for it would have to be so thick that they would ruin the effect of light and space.

But nothing seemed impossible for Anthemius. He solved the problem by setting the dome on halfdomes, so that the whole structure could rest on four widely spaced piers. Around the circumference of the dome were so many windows that the dome seemed to float over the church. Provincial visitors sometimes believed the story that the dome hung from heaven on a golden chain.

Anthemius had solved the impossible problem—at least, so it seemed. When Justinian finally entered the finished church, he looked up at a mosaic picture of Solomon. "Glory to God," said the emperor, "who has found me worthy to finish such a great work—surpassing even you, Solomon."

A few years later, the impossible dome fell down.

Even making the dome slightly taller didn't solve the structural problems. But the dome was too beautiful to give up on. When it was rebuilt for the last time, the builders took no chances. Exceptionally holy men came to spit some of their holiness into the mortar. A saint's relic was built into every twelfth course of bricks. And every brick was stamped with the initials of the verse, "God is in the midst of her; she shall not be moved."

Whether the reason was all that supernatural help or not, the dome stayed up. Earthquakes, sieges, and periods of neglect have taken their toll on the building, but with the help of occasional emergency repairs, the dome is still there today—though the building the Turks call Aya Sofia is now a state-run museum. The last liturgy was offered there in 1453. Afterward, the building was converted to a mosque.

4

Light in the Dark Ages

The West was certainly wounded badly by the fall of the Roman Empire. Civilization collapsed almost completely. Literacy, once common, was now a rare accomplishment. Culture itself was in danger of dying.

Only the Church had the structure and the resources to shore up the walls of civilization. And one man in particular made that his life's work.

Cassiodorus was a sixth-century nobleman who had a long career as a top minister in the court of Italy's barbarian king. But in his old age he went back to his hometown and set up a monastery—a monastery with a very specific purpose.

Throughout Italy, Cassiodorus saw civilization dying. A century and a half of invasions and wars had made books rare and educated readers rarer. The noblemen who had once kept large private libraries—and supported a profitable publishing industry—had largely been replaced by illiterate barbarian chieftains.

So Cassiodorus scooped up every book he could find from the ruined and abandoned libraries of Italy, and set his monks to work copying them. "Of all the fruits of manual labor," he said, "nothing pleases me as much as the work of the copyists—as long as they copy right."[1]

It was Cassiodorus who made copying books one of the monks' most important duties. "Every time you write one of the Lord's words, Satan is wounded,"[2] he used to say. After Cassiodorus, monasteries replaced the old private publishers all over western Europe. Monks continued to copy books through the darkest times of the Dark Ages and into the High Middle Ages, right up past the invention of the printing press. Cassiodorus had discovered the one sure way of preserving and safeguarding the wisdom of the past.

St. Benedict, Founder of Western Monasticism

The world was in chaos after the Roman Empire collapsed, so it's hardly surprising that many Christians decided to withdraw from it. Holy men had already been living as hermits in the East for some time, and the first monasteries also grew up in the East. The concept spread to the West, especially under the influence of St. Augustine. And as we just saw, Cassiodorus made monasteries into centers of learning. But the man who made monasticism a Western institution was Benedict of Nursia.

Benedict spent some time in Rome getting an education, but in about 500 he decided to get away from the world. He lived in a cave, but he wasn't alone for long. His example attracted others, and after a while there were a dozen monasteries surrounding his cave, each with a leader appointed by Benedict.

Benedict himself moved to Monte Cassino, where he founded the famous monastery there and established a rule for the communal life that became the model for all of western monasticism.

Benedict's rule was simple and reasonable. It didn't demand impossible feats of self-denial from the monks. Instead, the monks were to live simple and virtuous lives, and they were to give their time to devotion and useful work. Monasteries that followed this rule called themselves "Benedictine," and within a few years of St. Benedict's death in about 550, the Benedictine monks were spread all over western Christendom.

St. Benedict's sister, St. Scholastica, was also famous in her day as a leader of the monastic movement. She entered a convent near Monte Cassino, and once every year she and her brother would meet to talk about their work. In spite of the fact that they met so rarely, they must have been very close spiritually. St. Scholastica died a few years before St. Benedict; when he died, he was buried in the same grave as his sister.

GREGORY AND THE ANGELS

Britain, too, had been overrun by foreign invaders. The island had held out longer than most of the West, probably because of its strong leadership. Legend says that a Christian king named Arthur fought off the pagans, and there is good reason to believe that the legends were based on a real person.

But even Arthur could not put off the destruction forever. The people we know today as the English poured into Britain from northern Germany and the peninsula of Denmark, pushing the Christians back into the western mountains, into Wales. In the rest of Britain, the English takeover was so successful that the Latin and British languages disappeared completely. Pockets of Roman-British peasants still remained, and they may have been allowed to practice their Christian religion—but only because they were slaves, and the English conquerors didn't care about the religion of slaves.

The British Christians did not try to bring the good news to the pagan English. Instead, it was left for the Church of Rome to send missionaries. One day—so the story goes—an enthusiastic and popular Benedictine abbot named Gregory was walking through the Forum in Rome when he happened to see three light-haired slaves for sale. He was struck right away by their beauty.

"Where do those people come from?" he asked.

"They're Angles from Britain," the answer came back. The Angles were the barbarian tribe for whom England—Angleland—was named.

Gregory looked again at the beautiful slaves. "Not Angles, but angels," he remarked. When he heard that they were pagans, he thought it was a great pity that "people so graceful on the outside should not have grace on the inside."[3] At once he was seized by the idea of converting the English.

So he went to Pope Pelagius II and begged permission to make an expedition to England. The pope was very reluctant to let him go: Gregory had become one of the most popular men in Rome, and he was a natural leader. But it was hard to say no to such enthusiasm. The pope reluctantly gave his permission, and Gregory set off for Britain.

But Gregory never got there. When the people of Rome heard that he had left them, the pope had no peace. Everywhere he went, the pope was surrounded by crowds begging him to bring Gregory back. There were near riots in the streets. Worn down and unable to accomplish anything, the pope sent messengers running after Gregory and ordered him to come back to Rome.

So Gregory lost his chance to become a missionary. But he never forgot his plan to convert the English.

In 590, Pope Pelagius died of the plague that was ravaging Rome that year. The clergy and people of the city quickly chose Gregory as their new pope.

When Gregory heard that he had been elected, he was dismayed. It would be hard to imagine a more difficult time to be pope. The savage and heretical Lombards were doing their best to turn Italy into a wasteland, and the emperor's exarch (the Greek term for a governor) at Ravenna had given up and admitted that he could do nothing to protect Rome. The river Tiber had overflowed into the granaries and ruined Rome's food supply. The unsanitary conditions after the flood bred the epidemic that had killed Pope Pelagius. With all these disasters facing them at once, the people of Rome expected more than leadership from their new pope—they expected miracles. No wonder Gregory tried to run away!

For that was exactly what he did. He wanted to slip out of the city undetected, but the gates were all heavily guarded, and everyone knew what Gregory looked like. So he donned a disguise and persuaded some traveling salesmen to take him to a deserted forest. The disguise did him no good at all. Legend has it that wherever he tried to hide, a pillar of light hung over his head and gave him away. The people found him, seized him, and dragged him by force to St. Peter's, where—much against his will—he was consecrated bishop of Rome.

GREGORY THE EMPEROR-POPE

Gregory was a monk, the first monk ever chosen as pope. He had grown up in one of the few remaining old aristocratic families in Rome. Before taking his vows, he had been an important politician in the city, so he had some experience with administration. Nevertheless, he had never intended to become the most important politician of his age. Things just turned out that way. There was work to be done, and only Gregory could do it.

The invading Lombards were particularly vicious, at least to their enemies. They massacred everyone in their path, except for the few who might be useful as slaves. The Lombards who weren't pagans were Arians, so they had no qualms about plundering orthodox churches and slaughtering the clergy. Cities emptied as they approached, and soon Rome and Ravenna were the only substantial cities left in the northern half of Italy.

In theory, Italy was governed by the Roman emperor in Constantinople, through his exarch in Ravenna. In practice, the exarch was nearly powerless, and the empire in the East had enough of its own problems to worry about without defending Rome or Ravenna. With its naturally impenetrable defenses, the exarch might be able to hold on to Ravenna, but Rome was another matter. When the Lombards decided to march on Rome, no one was left to defend the once-proud city but Gregory.

It was fortunate for Rome that Gregory had experience in government as well as a deep and sincere faith. It took both qualities to save the city.

He led the people in prayers to end the plague; thousands joined him in a solemn procession. When they reached the tomb of Hadrian (one of the early Roman emperors), Gregory and many of the people saw a vision of the archangel Michael sheathing a flaming sword, indicating that the scourge was over. From that time on, the place has been known as the Castle of the Holy Angel—*Castel Sant'Angelo* in Italian.

The hapless exarch at Ravenna had declared that negotiating with the Lombards was impossible, but Gregory made peace with them when they reached the gates of Rome. In Constantinople, Emperor Maurice was angry at Gregory for behaving as if he were emperor. But, in fact, Maurice had been perfectly content to let Rome be wiped off the face of the earth. Every time Gregory had asked for his help, Maurice had been too busy with other important matters.

Having given Rome at least a temporary peace, Gregory had time to pursue his favorite dream: spreading the gospel to the barbarians. We'll hear more about his missions in a moment. For now, all we need to say is that thousands of pagans accepted the Catholic faith in Gregory's time.

GREGORY THE REFORMER

Gregory was not content to rest on his achievements, however. There was still work to be done.

The Mass was one of his most important concerns. Under Gregory it was revised and standardized, and Gregory himself wrote many of the hymns that have become part of our liturgical heritage. The form of music called "Gregorian chant" is probably named for him, because he set the standards for liturgical music for the next thousand years. (Gregory himself taught the chants to church choirs, beating out the time with a stick like a modern conductor.) Even today, much of our worship owes its shape to Gregory's reformed liturgy.

The finances of the Church also came under Gregory's eye. At the time, the Church owned huge estates. Gregory wanted the peasants who worked on these estates to be treated fairly, so he did his best to make legal guarantees that his successors would have to honor. When the Church spent money, Gregory wanted to make sure that everyone knew how it was being spent.

Finally, there was the clergy itself to keep in line. Many of the bishops were talented men from the old upper classes who had entered the Church because no other outlets for their ambition existed. Some thought they could act like irresponsible princes, living immoral lives and using their positions to get rich. Gregory wouldn't tolerate such abuses. He himself lived like a monk, and while he didn't try to force that lifestyle on all the clergy, he did at least insist on their living like Christians.

Gregory set the example for the popes who followed. Although few were as talented as Gregory, they all built on what he had accomplished. By default, they were the secular leaders in the city of Rome and the surrounding country, and they became more and more independent of the emperor in far-off Constantinople.

AUGUSTINE, THE RELUCTANT APOSTLE

Pope Gregory had never forgotten his hope of converting the English. Now that he was pope, he was in a position to do something about it. He gathered a group of monks to be his missionaries. One of them, who was named Augustine, was chosen as their leader; he would become bishop if the missionaries managed to establish a Christian community among the English. Gregory sent the missionaries off with his blessing and waited for news of the expedition.

Some time later, he was very surprised to see Augustine back in Rome. The monks had set off, but the closer they got to England, the more the mission had seemed like a very bad idea. The English were fierce and barbaric. And none of the monks even knew how to speak English. Wouldn't it be safer just to turn around and go home? So they stopped traveling and sent Augustine back to Rome to beg the pope for permission to come home.

Gregory had every right to be angry. Perhaps he was, but he didn't show it. Instead of a stern lecture, he gave Augustine encouragement. He wrote a letter for Augustine to take back to the group:

> Since it is better not to begin a good thing than to give up on it after you've begun, you really ought, my very dear sons, to finish the good work that, with the help of God, you've already begun. So don't let the hardship of the journey or the bad things people say deter you, but with all enthusiasm and all fervor complete what you've begun under God's direction—knowing that after great hardship comes a greater eternal reward.[4]

Either Pope Gregory's letter was really encouraging or the missionaries were too obedient to go home without permission. In 597, they reached Thanet, an island at the southeastern corner of England. It was the same island from which the English had launched their invasion of Britain about 150 years before. Now Augustine and his band of missionaries prepared a different kind of invasion.

WINNING BY PERSUASION

The idea that conversions could not be forced was the cardinal rule of Gregory's evangelism. He would do everything in his power to make Christianity attractive. For example, he told Augustine not to destroy the pagan temples in Britain; rather, he should set up Christian altars in the same places so that the people wouldn't have to change their habits to attend Christian worship. Any traditional pagan celebrations could be converted into Christian celebrations.

"The idol temples of that race should by no means be destroyed, but only the idols in them. Take holy water and sprinkle it in these shrines, build altars and place relics in them." Gregory told the missionaries to encourage the locals to continue slaughtering their animals, but not for sacrifice, for celebration and praise of God instead. "Thus while some outward rejoicings are preserved, they will be able more easily to share in inward rejoicings."

"It is doubtless impossible to cut out everything at once from their stubborn minds," Gregory said. "Just as the man who is attempting to climb to the highest place, rises by steps and degrees and not by leaps."[5]

Pope Gregory also made it clear that he would not tolerate persecution of the Jews. When he heard from some traveling Jewish merchants that Jews in southern Gaul had been forcibly baptized, he immediately sent a sharp condemnation to the bishops there for allowing it to happen. He censured the bishop of Terracina for banning the Jews there from a place where they usually held their festivals. When the bishop of Cagliari allowed a convert from Judaism to seize the local synagogue and turn it into a church, Gregory stepped in and ordered the building to be given back to the Jews.

For Gregory, the principle was always the same: only by peaceable persuasion can hearts be won for Christ. Even Gregory sometimes forgot that principle when he was dealing with the few pagans still left in Italy, and he had trouble applying it to heretics anywhere. But on the whole he set an example of tolerance and charity that won converts far more easily than any attempt at forced conversions.

From the Ruins of Rome

Gregory, Cassiodorus, Benedict, Augustine—the Church venerates their memory. They are a diverse group, representing different personalities, different concerns, and different approaches to the problems of their time. But history allows us to turn the lens as we look backward and see how each of their lives complemented the others. Together, these men succeeded, against all odds, in preserving and even developing the heritage of antiquity. If not for them, the fall of Rome would have brought far more dissolution than it did. Their network of monasteries and bishoprics proved quite hardy and kept working when many other governmental, military, and economic systems were breaking down.

When so many Christians could only lament the ruins and fallen stones of Rome's former glory, Gregory, Cassiodorus, Benedict, and Augustine had faith in the God who could "from these stones . . . raise up children to Abraham" (Luke 3:8). In a time of declining civic leadership and vanishing culture, God did indeed raise up Christians who could take those stones and build bridges so that Christians could carry the faith—and civilization—forward from one age to the next. 🪺

A Closer Look . . .

The Slave Who Civilized Ireland

Roman civilization never had much impact in Ireland. The empire had conquered the southern half of Britain, then stopped. The Irish were only barbarians as far as the Romans were concerned—simple natives to trade with or to fight off, depending on their mood.

By about the year 400, it was getting more difficult for the Romans to defend their far-off province of Britain. Taking advantage of the lax defenses, a band of Irish raiders made a sudden attack on northern Britain and carried off several people as slaves.

One of those slaves was a sixteen-year-old boy who would later be known as Patrick. The son of upper-class Romans, he had been raised as a Christian, but not a very sincere one. Now he found himself sold as a slave to a Druid priest in Ireland, where he spent his days tending sheep.

Shepherding is hard work, but it gave the youth long periods of time alone to think. "Every day I had to tend sheep," Patrick remembered later, "and I prayed many times a day. Love and fear of God gradually grew on me, and my faith got stronger and stronger. My spirit was so moved that I might say as many as a hundred prayers a day."[6]

Eventually he escaped from his Druid master and made his way back to his family in Britain. But then Patrick started to have dreams. He heard the voice of the Irish people calling him back. In spite of his years of slavery, he wanted only to bring the good news back to Ireland. And so he left his family once more, this time to be trained as a missionary by some of the greatest figures of the Church.

In 433, Patrick landed once again in Ireland. He knew he had a tough job ahead of him. One great saint, Palladius, had already given up on the Irish. But Patrick did not give up. In spite of constant danger to his own life, he made one convert after another. Soon there were Irish kings among his converts, and almost immediately men and women were attracted by Patrick's example to the monastic life. Monasteries sprouted up all over Ireland.

Today, St. Patrick is the patron of Ireland, remembered as the heroic missionary who brought Christianity to the island. But he brought more than Christianity—he brought civilization.

In most of the western Roman Empire, ordinary people could understand some form of Latin. But it was a foreign language to the Irish. Monks in the rest of Europe could be illiterate and ignorant and still, at least, understand the gospels in Latin. But Irish monks first had to learn to read and write a foreign language before they could read or hear the important texts of their faith.

Soon the Irish monks were the best-educated men in Europe. As the Dark Ages fell across the continent, Ireland kept the light of learning alive. Irish monks became the teachers of Europe, preserving the fragile flame of Roman civilization and spreading their knowledge all over the new barbarian kingdoms. When at last the darkness began to lift, Irish monks went to monasteries throughout Europe to teach the monks the wisdom that everyone but the Irish had almost forgotten.

5

Crusades Abroad and at Home

The Church in the West had survived the fall of Rome, and now it was the most powerful institution in Western Europe. But in the East, where the Church was born, the gradual erosion of the Byzantine Empire and the constant inroads of Islam threatened the very existence of Christianity.

Didn't the Church in the West owe something to the Christians of the East? Wasn't it the responsibility of all Christians to come to the aid of their brothers and sisters in distress?

That was the question that launched the crusades.

In the Middle East, whose history spans thousands of years, the crusades seem as fresh as yesterday's headlines. And the same religious feelings that fueled both sides of the medieval wars are still with us today. Jerusalem—which has never been a very large city—is still, in world politics, probably the most important spot on the globe.

Today it's easy to portray the crusades as a simple act of Christian aggression against the innocent and bewildered Muslims; or, alternatively, as a desperate last-ditch defense of Christianity against the relentless drive of the Islamic forces. Both portrayals are wrong. There was aggression on both sides, sincere religious zeal on both sides, and a surprising amount of respect for the other on both sides. There was also simple greed and avarice on both sides, and sometimes the greed managed to pervert the religious zeal.

CHRISTIANS PERSECUTED IN THE EAST

From the time of the Apostles, there had been four great centers of Christianiy in the wold: Jerusalem, Antioch, Alexandria, and Rome. They were called "Patriarchates" because their churches were governed by patriarchal archbishops. Of those four cities, three were now in Muslim control. And still the Muslim Empire pushed outward. By 732, Islamic forces were invading France—and set on Rome—when Charles Martel decisively turned them back at the Battle of Poitiers.

In the centuries that followed, Christians in the East lived as second-class citizens under the caliphate, the giant Muslim Empire that ruled the East. Christians were prohibited from any public expression of their faith that would offend Muslim eyes or ears, such as church bells or street processions. They also were not allowed to interfere in any way with the conversion of Christians to Islam. Nor could they encourage any Muslims to convert to Christianity. Christians were taxed heavily, and the practice of certain professions was often forbidden to them. But as long as they kept to these restrictions, Christians were allowed to worship in their own way.

However, the Islamic rulers did extend a welcome to Christian pilgrims. Pilgrims brought money, and a devout Muslim understood and respected the idea of a pilgrimage, since pilgrimages are so important to the Islamic faith.

Eventually the caliphate fell apart, and the rulers, known as caliphs, were reduced to figureheads with no real power. In the civil wars that followed the collapse of the empire, the fanatical Hakim, sultan of Egypt, gained control of Palestine. In 1009, Hakim launched the most intense persecution of Christians in the East since Diocletian's reign of terror in the late third century. He demolished all the beautiful churches in Jerusalem, including the massive Church of the Holy Sepulchre, which was left a forlorn ruin.

Hakim soon tired of his persecution. Possibly he feared retaliation by the Italian naval powers, which by this time had grown in power and had to be taken into consideration, even from Hakim's location in the eastern Mediterranean. Once again, pilgrims were allowed to flock to Jerusalem, though now the Muslim rulers charged them an admission fee at the gate.

Under Hakim's successor Al Mustansir, the Church of the Holy Sepulchre was rebuilt in 1037. The Byzantine emperor was given the privilege of paying for the reconstruction, but only after first releasing five thousand Muslim captives. One Muslim traveler who went to Jerusalem in 1047 wrote that "every year huge numbers of people from Rome [meaning the Byzantine Empire] visit the Church of the Holy Sepulchre. . . . It can hold eight thousand people."[1]

But this respite lasted only for a short time. When the Turks—who were recent converts to Islam—captured Jerusalem, they brought with them a fanaticism even worse than Hakim's. They enslaved the Christians of Palestine and viewed foreign pilgrims as nothing more than infidel pests.

Yet even then, the stream of Christian pilgrims didn't stop. The Turks might beat them, imprison them, enslave them, or even kill them, but still the pilgrims arrived. The more dangerous the journey, the more worthwhile it seemed. And if the pilgrims were killed, then they would die as martyrs. The survivors returned home to show off their scars, and their stories inspired still more pilgrimages.

More than once, a pope or an emperor had conceived a plan to rescue Palestine from the Turks, but nothing came of those schemes. Meanwhile, two-thirds of the world's Christian lands had fallen to the Muslim sword. By 1095 it was clear that, unless Christians united to halt the aggression, the remaining Christian lands would soon be overrun.

That was certainly clear to the Byzantine emperor Alexius Comnenus, who put aside Constantinople's strained relations with Rome and begged Pope Urban II for help. The pope was moved by his plea. Moreover, he saw this as an opportunity to heal the schism that had occurred in 1054 between the Christian East and West. Urban summoned both churchmen and statesmen to an unusual council at Clermont, France. There he preached a rousing call for action both spiritual and military—a campaign to defend Christendom against Muslim aggression, to help the persecuted Christians in Eastern lands, and to reclaim the Holy Sepulchre. The Christian soldiers would take a vow and wear a red cross (thus the name "crusade," from the Latin word *crux,* meaning "cross"). They would receive a plenary indulgence for their efforts to fulfill their vow.

The councilors at Clermont received Urban's preaching with tremendous enthusiasm, crying *"Deus vult!"*—"God wills it!"

OFF TO THE HOLY LAND

Enthusiasm for a crusade spread rapidly. Preachers spread the word in the streets and the countryside. Crowds formed and set off toward the Holy Land, having no idea how they would get there.

These crowds consisted not of trained and disciplined soldiers, but of every class of people, from peasants to kings. Nobles who had everything to lose and nothing to gain—on earth at least—set out for the seemingly mythical lands of the East without a moment's hesitation. Peasants left their plows in the fields, and masons left their buildings half-completed.

One of the early enthusiasts of the crusade, Peter the Hermit, led a huge army of assorted pilgrims, and reached the Holy Land before any of the professional soldiers. This "People's Crusade" was easily routed. Thousands were slaughtered in their first brave encounter with the Turks; the ragged remnant, including Peter, hobbled back to Constantinople to await the arrival of the professionals. Though it may have ended in defeat, the People's Crusade" showed just how much Christians were willing to sacrifice to recover the holy places. Crusading was a genuine popular movement, and it was truly religious at heart.

The professionals themselves, who had agreed to meet at Constantinople, were a patchwork of nobles, most of them Franks. Their names have come down to us almost as legendary figures. There was crafty Bohemond; the cowardly Stephen of Blois; Raymond of Saint-Gilles, the brilliant but quick-tempered general; and Godfrey of Bouillon, the romantic hero. With them came tens of thousands of knights and soldiers.

Emperor Alexius was amazed and appalled. He had hoped Pope Urban would send a small professional army. Instead, a mob seemed to be camped outside the walls of Constantinople. From the start, the Greeks and the Franks did not get along. The Franks resented the crafty refinement of the Greeks, who they saw as experts at devising loopholes that rendered bargains null and void. The Greeks thought the Franks were smelly barbarians who were uncontrollably violent.

Nevertheless, Alexius knew he couldn't afford to have the Franks as his enemies. Whenever quarrels broke out, he tried to patch them up. He finally reached an agreement with the crusaders. He would send his best guides, and he would join them with his entire army later; in return, they would swear allegiance to him, and all the lands they conquered—which had formerly belonged to the empire—would revert to the empire again.

Unfortunately, the emperor's best guide, the general Taticius, turned out to be no help at all. It wasn't his fault: he took the best route through Asia Minor. But the Turks knew that route, and they had burned the fields and poisoned the wells all along the way. The crusaders were starving, and of course they blamed Taticius. Nevertheless, after almost incredible hardships, they reached the great city of Antioch, which Emperor Alexius hoped would soon be safely under the sway of Constantinople again.

THE TWO SIEGES OF ANTIOCH

Whoever controlled Antioch would control Palestine. It was the strategic key to the whole eastern Mediterranean. If the crusaders were to succeed in taking Jerusalem, they would have to take Antioch first.

Yet it seemed impossible. Antioch was still a great city, bigger than any city in western Europe and formerly the second-largest city of the Byzantine Empire. The Muslims had equipped it with all the latest defense technology, and the crusaders didn't have nearly enough soldiers to surround the place. They could block the major highways, but Antioch could still get supplies and even soldiers through the mountains behind the city.

There were several circumstances that favored the crusaders.

The emir of Antioch, Yaghi-Siyan, had made enemies of the nearest Muslim princes, so any help would have to come from a long way off. He also seems to have been somewhat cowardly: the arrival of the Christian army threw him into a panic, and his hesitation gave them time to set up their siege unmolested. In addition, most of the peasants in the surrounding countryside were still Christian, and they helped the crusaders when they could. The people of Antioch, too, were largely Christian.

Still, the crusaders endured severe hardships for some time. No additional reinforcement had come from the Byzantine emperor, so in the winter cold, they were nearly starving. Morale was dismally low, and many of the crusaders were still inclined to blame the Byzantine general Taticius for all their problems. Fearing their wrath, Taticius secretly left with his small squadron of Byzantine mercenaries, and before long he was back in Constantinople.

This made the crusaders even more furious. One thing was certain: if this was how Alexius' general and right-hand man treated them, then they didn't owe the emperor anything. When they did take Antioch, it would be for themselves, not for the emperor.

And take it they did, after eight months of a grueling siege. As soon as the crusaders appeared in the streets, the native population welcomed them as liberators. The Turks were attacked by the thousands. The cowardly emir Yaghi-Siyan, seeing Frankish flags flying from the walls, hopped on his horse and galloped away as fast as he could. The next day local peasants brought his head to the crusaders. He may have had a greater chance of surviving if he had been captured by the Franks instead of by the natives.

Antioch, where the followers of the Way were first called Christians (see Acts 11:26), was in Christian hands again.

Immediately, however, the Franks were themselves besieged by the Muslim reinforcements who had arrived too late to prevent the capture of the city. The crusaders were in even worse shape than before.

Then something extraordinary happened. A servant of one of the nobles claimed to have a vision that led him to discover a hidden relic—the Holy Lance that had pierced Christ's side. When the man emerged from digging, with the iron object in hand, suddenly the entire crusader army had new life. God was on their side, and victory was certain. Once again, we see how much the crusade was a religious movement. The crusaders believed they were doing God's work. They weren't surprised by miracles—in fact, they expected miracles.

Emboldened, the crusaders made a daring and successful attack on the Muslim army outside the walls of Antioch that nearly wiped them out. The Muslim survivors ran off to spread the rumor that nothing would stop these Franks.

ON TO JERUSALEM

Now that they had succeeded in Antioch, the crusaders began marching to Jerusalem, leaving behind a Frankish Christian prince in Antioch.

There were only a few thousand soldiers, along with the ragged band of poor people who had few weapons more sophisticated than sticks. But their reputation was powerful. Since they had captured the great city of Antioch, the crusaders looked invincible to the petty Muslim lords who stood between them and Jerusalem. Some of the emirs even gave the crusaders guides and money in return for their promise to keep marching.

The nobles were by now quarreling among themselves over who should hold power; but, as the crusaders came closer and closer to Jerusalem, they were filled with more and more enthusiasm. All around them were scenes from the life of Christ. It seemed as if the whole country had turned out to welcome them. Most of the Muslims had run away when they heard the crusaders were coming, so everywhere the crusaders saw only Christians—Christians who told them tales of Muslim cruelty.

At last, four years after Pope Urban had proclaimed the crusade, the crusaders wept as they caught their first glimpse of Jerusalem.

Here it was at last, the very place where Christ had suffered, died, and risen from the dead for the world's salvation.

It's impossible to describe the emotional effect on the crusaders at the sight of Jerusalem. All the events of Christ's passion came vividly to their minds. Yet here were the historic churches, desecrated and turned into mosques. They were outraged.

The siege of Jerusalem lasted less than six weeks. The Muslim defenders had stripped the surrounding countryside of supplies, had poisoned all the wells, and—learning a lesson from Antioch, perhaps—had thrown all the Christians out of the city. The crusaders had nothing to eat and were soon weak from thirst and hunger. Yet their sufferings only strengthened their resolve. God might test them, but they were sure he was on their side.

The crusaders marched barefoot around the city, carrying crosses, praying, and singing—behavior that the Muslim soldiers ridiculed. To taunt the Christians, the soldiers pilfered crosses from all the churches in Jerusalem and made obscene displays with them on the city walls. If the crusaders needed any more provocation, these insults to Christ's cross settled the matter.

On July 15, 1099, the crusaders fought their way into the city. In a few hours, they had crushed all resistance.

Then the generals lost control. The army had suffered and had seen the cross desecrated; nothing the barons did could restrain their mad fury. They stormed through the streets, slaughtering everyone they encountered. Tancred, one of the barons, placed hundreds of Arab soldiers and Jews under his protection on the roof of a mosque; but the mob fought their way past Tancred's banners and butchered everyone. The bloodbath lasted two days. There were no non-Christian survivors in the city.

The massacre in Jerusalem was the foulest stain on what had begun as a sincerely Christian enterprise. It was what might be expected of warfare in the Middle Ages: Muslims had done the same to Christians before and would do so again. Indeed, Christians had done the same to Christians, and Muslims to Muslims. Still, it certainly was not what Pope Urban had intended when he issued the call for a crusade.

RESULTS OF THE FIRST CRUSADE

In spite of its failures, however, the First Crusade produced astonishing results. Jerusalem was a Christian city again, and that was the goal of the entire enterprise. Two other Christian states had been established, at Edessa and Antioch. And ordinary Christian citizens—not just kings and generals—could see what their zeal might accomplish in the temporal order.

But holding on to these new possessions would be difficult. The crusaders had been fortunate—they had shown up just when the local Muslim princes had been at their most divided and disorganized. With a little more cooperation, the Muslims might have succeeded in keeping the crusaders out or in throwing them out. The native Christians, too, began to grumble at the western Christians, who seemed to regard them as heretics.

To survive at all, the rulers of the crusader states had to learn to adapt to local conditions—to get rid of some of their deepest prejudices and make the most of what they had. For the next century and a half, the crusaders' kingdoms in Palestine and Syria would live precariously, surrounded by Muslims who were sometimes allies and sometimes enemies. They would always be looking for more help from the West to shore up their defenses.

By the middle 1100s, the crusader states had turned into something unique in the world. The Franks were still just as passionately attached to the Latin Church, but they nevertheless allowed Muslims and Eastern Christians complete equality. They had learned the lesson the rest of the world is still struggling with today: how to practice tolerance and be friendly with other faiths without lapsing into indifference. Strange as it may seem, under the crusaders—those fiery religious fanatics who had come thousands of miles to put the infidel in his place—the Middle East had turned into an oasis of religious freedom.

But it was not to last. Just when the crusader kingdoms were making progress, Europe lost interest in crusading. More crusades would come and go; some of the later crusades would turn against Christians rather than against Muslims. Eventually, the crusader states vanished, and Palestine and Syria were ruled by Muslims again. They continued to be ruled by Muslims until European colonial powers took them over in the 1800s.

FERDINAND AND ISABELLA

For the people of medieval Spain, the word "crusade" meant something different from what it meant for the rest of Europe. Spaniards carried on their *cruzado* steadily, unrelentingly for eight centuries. Spain had fallen to Islamic rule in the 700s, during the first tidal wave of Muslim expansion; but the people steadily resisted conversion to Islam. In spite of the usual incentives to convert—and disincentives to persevere—they held to their Christian faith, and the people in formerly disparate regions found new unity in their persecuted status. They began to think of themselves as one nation.

Against all odds, Spain's Christian population maintained their identity, their faith, and, most remarkably, their momentum over centuries when they measured their gains in the smallest increments. The Spaniards called this process—this slow and steady recovery of their lands—the *reconquista*, or "reconquest."

This crusade was different from all the others. The Spaniards did not have to leave home in order to fight for the recovery of Christian lands and the rescue of Christian people. Moreover, Spain's crusading ardor—unlike that of its European neighbors—never faded. Spain knew only too well the consequences of defeat.

By 1469 many of the lands of Spain had been regained for Christianity, and most Muslims had been driven south to the kingdom of Granada. Islam was now very much on the defensive and in retreat. Then, in that year, the most important wedding in a thousand years took place. At the time, everyone knew it was important, of course—it involved a prince and a princess. But no one knew that the marriage of Isabella of Castile to Ferdinand of Aragon would completely change the history of the world for centuries to come.

Isabella was heiress to the throne of Castile; Ferdinand was heir to the throne of Aragon. When they came into their inheritances, the two Christian kingdoms of Spain were united, and Spain suddenly became a power to reckon with in Europe.

That in itself might have been only a small change. Powers rise and fall in Europe; they did then, and they still do now. What made this union different was that both Isabella and Ferdinand were amazingly able and ambitious rulers. Once they decided on a course of action, it happened. And from the beginning, they decided that Spain must become a great Christian empire.

First Ferdinand and Isabella had to unite Spain. Until their reign, Spain had been overrun by armed nobles warring against one another. The new king and queen put a stop to the problem by requiring that the nobles acknowledge their authority. They also destroyed the castles of the nobles who had been terrorizing the countryside.

The next order of business was to drive the Muslims from southern Spain. The kingdom of Granada was much smaller than it had been at the height of Islamic power, but it was still a prosperous country with about three million people and was a constant thorn in the side of Christian Spain. At just the right moment, Granada picked a fight, and Ferdinand and Isabella took advantage of the occasion to begin the reconquest of the South. Methodically taking town after town, they reduced the kingdom bit by bit until only the capital city of Granada itself remained. Ferdinand and Isabella themselves led the siege on the city. They refused to fight a pitched battle; instead, they patiently waited until the city's inhabitants began to starve. In full view of the people, Ferdinand and Isabella built a suburb of their own, with streets and permanent buildings. They called it Santa Fe—"Holy Faith." The effect on morale in the city was devastating: the king and queen were showing that they were absolutely determined to stay. Finally, the city accepted Ferdinand's offer of honorable surrender. In the year 1492, all of Spain was finally Christian again. The last Muslim kingdom had been expelled from western Europe.

Of course, the year 1492 is familiar to any American for another reason. In that same year, Ferdinand and Isabella financed the expedition of a brilliant and persuasive sea captain named Christopher Columbus, who had a scheme to find the Indies by sailing west instead of east. If a better route to the Indies could be found—one not controlled by the Turks or the Portuguese—then Spain would suddenly become what today we would call an economic superpower. Columbus might never make it, but the risk of three ships was worth it in view of the riches that would pour in if Columbus succeeded in his venture.

Yet just as the Spanish *cruzado* was coming to an end, a new challenge was coming from within Christendom itself.

A Closer Look. . .

St. Francis Preaches to the Birds

This is a very old story about St. Francis, written down when there were still people alive who knew him.[2] St. Francis loved all God's creation, and he felt that love for even the tiniest of God's creatures.

And as he went on his way, with great fervor, St. Francis lifted up his eyes, and saw on some trees by the wayside a great multitude of birds; and being much surprised, he said to his companions, "Wait for me here by the way, while I go and preach to my little sisters the birds."

Entering the field, he began to preach to the birds on the ground, and suddenly all those on the trees came around him as well. They all listened while St. Francis preached to them, and did not fly away until he had given them his blessing. And Brother Masseo related afterwards to Brother James of Massa how St. Francis went among them and even touched them with his garments, and how none of them moved.

Now the substance of the sermon was this: "My little sisters the birds, you owe much to God, your Creator, and you ought to sing his praise at all times and in all places, because he has given you liberty to fly about into all places. And though you neither spin nor sew, he has given you a twofold and a threefold clothing for yourselves and for your offspring. Two of all your species he sent into the ark with Noah that you might not be lost to the world. Besides which, he feeds you, though you neither sow nor reap. He has given you fountains and rivers to quench your thirst, mountains and valleys in which to take refuge, and trees in which to build your nests. Your Creator loves you much, having thus favored you with such bounties. Beware, my little sisters, of the sin of ingratitude, and study always to give praise to God."

As he said these words, all the birds began to open their beaks, to stretch their necks, to spread their wings, and reverently to bow their heads to the ground, endeavoring by their motions and by their songs to manifest their joy to St. Francis. And the saint rejoiced with them. He wondered to see such a multitude of birds, and was charmed with their beautiful variety, with their attention and familiarity, for all of which he devoutly gave thanks to the Creator.

Having finished his sermon, St. Francis made the sign of the cross, and gave them leave to fly away. Then all those birds rose up into the air, singing most sweetly; and, following the sign of the cross, which St. Francis had made, they divided themselves into four companies. One company flew toward the East, another toward the West, one toward the South, and one toward the North; each company as it went singing most wonderfully, signifying thereby, that as St. Francis, the bearer of the cross of Christ, had preached to them and made upon them the sign of the cross, after which they had divided among themselves the four parts of the world, so the preaching of the cross of Christ, renewed by St. Francis, would be carried by him and by his brethren over all the world, and that the humble friars, like little birds, should posses nothing in this world, but should cast all the care of their lives on the providence of God.

The Universal Doctor and the Dumb Ox

Albert the Great, or Albertus Magnus in Latin, was certainly one of the great thinkers of all time. He was known as *Doctor Universalis*–the Universal Doctor–because he wrote about almost everything–theology, ethics, science, philosophy (he was one of the first to make popular the newly rediscovered works of Aristotle), logic, and metaphysics. In fact, the German Dominican might have been remembered as the greatest thinker of the Middle Ages if he hadn't been surpassed by one of his own pupils.

In about 1245, Albert was teaching at Paris. One of his students was particularly quiet; his fellow students thought he must be rather stupid, and they called him "the dumb ox." But one day, when he finally did speak up in class, his thoughts were so clear and brilliant that Albert was amazed. "You call him a dumb ox," Albert told the rest of the class, "but let me tell you, some day this ox will bellow so loud that the whole world will hear him."

The student was Thomas Aquinas, a young Dominican who had faced serious opposition to join the order–so serious that his family had kidnapped him and kept him imprisoned for a year when he refused to change his mind. But Thomas was stubborn. He was also brilliant, as Albert found out. The teacher and the student became lifelong friends.

Thomas, too, had encountered the philosopher Aristotle, and he agreed with Albert that the clear reasoning of the philosopher could be a great help to Christian theology. He quickly rose to be one of the great intellectual figures of his time, writing an amazing number of important theological works. He sometimes worked on more than one book at once, keeping multiple secretaries in the room, and walking to one or the other as an idea for this book or that occurred to him.

In about 1265, Thomas began work on what would be his greatest legacy to the Church, the *Summa Theologica*. It was to be a compendium of all theology and doctrine, using the methods of Aristotle to expound the principles of the Christian faith. He had finished most of it by 1273, when he suddenly stopped.

On the night of December 6, 1273, Thomas had an amazing vision from heaven. When he awoke, he announced, "I can't do any more. After the secrets I've seen, everything I've written seems like nothing but straw." Thomas died a few months later, in March of 1274; some of his students completed the *Summa* from Thomas' outline, using bits and pieces of other things Thomas had written.

In 1277, some of Thomas' writings were condemned at the University of Paris. His old teacher, Albert the Great, had been living in retirement at Cologne, but—old though he was—he would not let the challenge to his beloved friend's philosophy go unmet. He set out at once for Paris to defend Thomas, and—more important—the idea he and Thomas shared that faith was not opposed to reason.

Since then, both men have been recognized as saints. The philosophy of St. Thomas Aquinas has served as the intellectual backbone of Catholicism, and his principle that faith and reason are not contradictory is the recognized doctrine of the whole Church.

6

Reformation Inside and Out

Martin Luther was a troubled young man who seriously worried about going to hell. He was obsessed with the idea that he was a sinner unworthy of salvation. He became an Augustinian friar and subjected himself to the most rigorous asceticism. But nothing was enough; he realized that even his good works came only from the selfish desire to avoid damnation, not from love of God.

It wasn't until Luther was reading the epistles of Paul that he overcame his despair. From reading Paul, he concluded that faith is what justifies a person before God, not works. So far he was at least arguably orthodox, and Luther's struggle might have remained a personal one if St. Peter's Basilica in Rome hadn't been in such disrepair.

The basilica had been built by the emperor Constantine, so it was well over a thousand years old. Earthquakes had made it unstable, and centuries of battles around Rome had left their marks. In 1506, Pope Julius II decided it would have to be entirely replaced. The new basilica would be the most magnificent church ever built, if the pope had his way (and in fact many historians of architecture would say that he did have his way). Ultimately it took one hundred years, thirteen architects, and twenty popes to finish the building.

A building project on that scale requires massive amounts of money, and Pope Julius decided to offer an indulgence to anyone who contributed to the cause.

Properly, an indulgence removes the temporal punishment

of a sin that has already been forgiven. However, the wandering preachers who went to every corner of western Europe to raise money for St. Peter's tended to exaggerate and simplify the nature of indulgences. They left some people with the impression that one could buy an indulgence that would instantly release a deceased loved one from purgatory.

Luther was furious. He viewed this practice as an attack on the doctrine of justification by faith. On October 31, 1517, he tacked up an invitation to a public debate on the subject—set out in ninety-five statements or "theses."

It's likely that Luther intended only to provoke a debate. But that new invention, the printing press, spread the Ninety-Five Theses all over Germany with incredible speed.

Some of Luther's propositions were orthodox; some were heretical; some were dubious. All were inflammatory, and soon all Germany—and much of the rest of the continent—was talking about the Augustinian friar and his theses.

The Church didn't condemn Luther right away. Pope Leo X, who had succeeded Julius II, was hoping that Frederick the Wise, a powerful noble from Saxony, would be elected emperor, and Frederick the Wise had taken an interest in Luther and sometimes intervened on his behalf. As long as there was a chance that Frederick would be elected, the pope found it expedient not to displease Frederick. But Frederick lost the election. Luther, meanwhile, encouraged by the favorable reception of his ideas, was turning away from Rome more and more. When Leo finally excommunicated him in 1521, he burned the bull of excommunication and defied the pope.

Then German politics came into play. At an imperial diet held at Worms, Charles V, the recently elected emperor, declared that he would defend the Catholic faith with the last ounce of his power. Luther responded that he would not recant. Luther left just before the diet issued an edict declaring him an outlaw.

Since the various princes of Germany were always squabbling, they saw in the Luther issue a new weapon to use against their adversaries. In a very short time, some of the more important German states had declared their support for Luther—and his friend Frederick. In doing so, they placed themselves outside the Catholic Church.

Luther, meanwhile, repudiated his monastic vows, and the Lutherans (as his followers had become known) declared that all monastic vows were worthless. In some places, mobs of men raided convents, "liberating" the nuns for marriage. In 1526, Luther himself married a former nun.

Luther publicly applauded the princes who employed violent means to enforce his heresy—"utterly destroying the abominations and scandals of the Roman pestilence."[1] Many common folk heard his words as a call to arms. A Lutheran mob descended on Rome in 1527, sacking the city, desecrating churches, raping the women, and torturing Catholic men, women, and children.

At another diet in Augsburg in 1530, the Lutherans presented a complete exposition of their positions. They claimed that they were truly Catholic, that they continued to reverence the Mass, and that they desired only the freedom to worship in the way their consciences dictated. Behind the scenes, many people on both sides were working for a reunion. Philipp Melanchthon, a mild-mannered theologian who became the voice of reason among the Lutherans, had drawn up the "Augsburg Confession," and many on the Catholic side also hoped some compromise could be reached.

But Luther's doctrines were growing more heretical with time. He stubbornly referred to the pope as the "Antichrist" and rejected all but two of the seven sacraments. His former emphasis on faith developed into a dogmatic insistence on "faith alone, apart from works," a principle that contradicted both Scripture and tradition. (He inserted the word "alone" into Romans 3:28, about justification by faith, when he translated the New Testament). Luther established himself with the same authority that he had denied the popes. He even went so far as to approve polygamy for a nobleman who had tired of his first wife. The pope saw little chance for reconciliation.

With the princes involved to such a degree, war was the inevitable result—a fierce religious war that lasted until the Peace of Augsburg in 1555 divided Germany into Catholic and Protestant camps. *Cuius regio, eius religio* was the principle of the agreement: whoever was the ruler in each state would decide the religion. It wasn't a declaration of tolerance. It was simply a blanket permission for Catholic princes to suppress Protestants and for Protestant princes to suppress Catholics.

HENRY VIII SECEDES

In England, King Henry VIII professed himself shocked by the Lutheran revolt. He wrote a treatise against Luther's doctrine of the sacraments. Henry was a well-educated man, and his little book was so good that Pope Leo X gave him the title defender of the Church—a title the English monarchs have tenaciously clung to ever since.

But Henry had trouble at home. He was married to Catherine of Aragon, but she had borne him no male heirs who survived infancy. Meanwhile, Henry had grown attracted to a woman named Anne Boleyn, a lady-in-waiting at his court. He might have made her his mistress in the ordinary royal way, but she refused to have anything to do with him unless she could be queen. Henry's only recourse was to get rid of Catherine of Aragon, which meant having his marriage annulled. Unfortunately for the king, Pope Clement VII couldn't see any reason why the marriage was invalid. Henry tried stubbornly for some time to convince the pope, but when he found it couldn't be done, he decided to deny the pope's authority. His friend Thomas Cranmer was installed as archbishop of Canterbury, and in 1533, Cranmer, a man who was easily bullied, declared the marriage invalid. In 1534, by the Act of Supremacy, Henry declared himself the supreme head of the Church of England. All the clergy and all the government officials were required to take an oath that they would accept the new law.

Sir Thomas More, Henry's former chancellor, refused to take the oath and was beheaded, earning his place in the lists of martyred saints. He had been appointed to the chancellorship to replace Cardinal Wolsey, who had failed to get Henry's divorce approved. But More could not justify the divorce either. It was typical of More that he resigned quietly rather than making a scene. He could not, however, agree to admit King Henry as the head of the Church, and so he was convicted of treason and beheaded. "You will give me today a greater benefit than ever any mortal man can be able to give me," he told his executioner. "Pluck up your spirits, man, and be not afraid to do your office. My neck is very short: take heed, therefore, that you strike not awry for saving of your honesty."[2] Then, just before the blade fell, he moved his beard out of the way, explaining that at least the beard had never offended the king.

Having declared his independence from the pope, Henry at first tried to maintain his hold on Catholic tradition. He continued to reject Lutheran ideas, and he retained traditional Catholic devotions and liturgy. But the monasteries remained stubborn supporters of the pope, and Henry found a theological justification for dissolving them all and turning their treasuries over to his own treasury. The buildings were either given to Henry's friends to be used as palaces or left to decay.

Meanwhile, Henry took several more wives, resorting to divorce or execution when he tired of them. Without the Church to protect them, these women were subject to the whims of the self-proclaimed head of the National Church. In 1547, Henry died, having married a total of six times. His sickly son Edward (born to Jane Seymour, Henry's third wife) inherited the throne, and Archbishop Cranmer soon turned the Church of England (or Anglican Church) more toward Lutheranism. The new religion was imposed with brutal severity.

Edward died in 1553, and his half sister Mary (Henry's daughter by Catherine of Aragon, his first wife) became queen. She revoked the Act of Supremacy and restored the Catholic Church to England. English Protestants called her "Bloody Mary" because she presided over the execution of three hundred Protestants.

When Mary died in 1558, her half sister Elizabeth I (daughter of Henry VIII and Anne Boleyn), who was no less bloody, yanked England back in the other direction again. Queen Elizabeth restored Protestantism and announced a new Act of Supremacy over the Church of England. Parliament declared it a felony to go to Mass. Once firmly established in her reign, Elizabeth executed harsh judgment against Catholics. John Nelson, a

Jesuit priest who refused to take Elizabeth's oath of supremacy, was drawn on a hurdle from Newgate to Tyburn, where he was hanged, disemboweled, and quartered. Such gruesome executions were fairly routine. In the British Isles, Catholics would be persecuted for centuries to come.

It's estimated that more than six hundred men and women died as martyrs for the Catholic faith in post-Reformation England.

SPLITS AND MORE SPLITS

The Lutherans and the Anglicans tried to retain some semblance of traditional Christian doctrine and worship. But if—as Luther claimed—the individual interpretation of Scripture was to be the only standard for Christianity, then the result was predictable. Other sects arose, and soon Protestants were split into dozens of sects and subsects, each one based on a particular interpretation of Scripture—often just a few verses in Scripture.

One of the most influential Protestant thinkers was John Calvin. He taught that there was no free will at all. From the very beginning, God had chosen certain people to be saved and others to be damned, and there was nothing one could do about it. "We say, then, that Scripture clearly proves this much," Calvin asserted, "that God by his eternal and immutable counsel determined once for all those whom it was his pleasure one day to admit to salvation, and those whom, on the other hand, it was his pleasure to doom to destruction. We maintain that this counsel, as regards the elect, is founded on his free mercy, without any respect to human worth, while those whom he dooms to destruction are excluded from access to life by a just and blameless, but at the same time incomprehensible judgment."[3]

Calvinism spread through much of Europe, including southern France, the Netherlands, and Scotland. In Geneva, the followers of Calvin set up a repressive Calvinist theocracy. The Presbyterian Church, based on Calvinist principles, ultimately became the national church of Scotland, and remains so today. In France, the Calvinists were called Huguenots.

Another influential sect was the Anabaptists, who believed that a Christian must be fully aware of the decision he or she is making before being baptized. Infant baptisms, therefore, were invalid, and a true Christian must be baptized again. The Anabaptists' descendants are known today as Baptists.

Many of these sects turned viciously iconoclastic, destroying centuries of priceless art to combat what they viewed as image-worship. The Lutherans had not worried about sacred images, but other sects came to abhor them as works of the devil. In England, the great shrine of St. Thomas à Becket was utterly destroyed. Calvinist mobs rampaged through southern France, throwing stones at statues. All throughout northern Europe, great cathedrals still bear the damage inflicted by the iconoclasts.

By the 1600s, the Protestants were putting as much effort into condemning each other as they were into condemning Rome. Through the 1800s, the history of Protestant Christianity is mostly a history of small sects splitting into even smaller sects.

IGNATIUS LOYOLA AND THE NEW KNIGHTHOOD

Ignatius Loyola—in Spanish, Iñigo Lopez de Loyola—was born in 1491 in the Basque province of Spain. As a member of the minor nobility, he naturally ended up as a soldier. In 1521, he was wounded in battle and faced a long recovery. Bored and desperate for something to read, Ignatius asked for some knightly romances to pass the time. There weren't any in the home where Ignatius was recuperating—only saints' lives and a popular life of Christ—so he read these. As he read, he noticed something: he felt real and lasting joy when he imagined himself in the role of some saint, but only a transient pleasure when he thought about the chivalry that used to obsess him.

When he finally recovered in 1522, Ignatius decided to act on his discovery. He would no longer be an ordinary knight and warrior; instead he would be a knight in the service of Christ. He made a pilgrimage to Montserrat, and there, adapting the knightly custom of the vigil, he set his sword on the altar of the Blessed Virgin and watched all night, dedicating himself to her service.

For eleven years, Ignatius studied, hoping to prepare himself to serve the Church. Finally, in 1534, he was ready to begin his mission—although he still wasn't entirely sure what that mission would be.

By this time, Ignatius had gathered a group of like-minded friends around him, and on August 15, 1534, the group took vows of poverty, chastity, and loyalty to the pope. They also vowed to make—if possible—a pilgrimage to the Holy Land. The friends called their group the Society of Jesus.

Wars made the pilgrimage impossible, but in 1539 Ignatius received Pope Paul III's approval for his new order.

The Society of Jesus was something drastically new. Its members, known as "Jesuits," were spiritual soldiers in the service of the pope. They were to be ready to go anywhere the pope asked and to do whatever he required of them, without question. Ignatius insisted on strict discipline and first-rate education; a Jesuit could answer any argument against the faith that was presented to him. As we'll soon see, the Jesuits were superb missionaries. They also fought against the spread of Protestantism. When Protestant nations like England were killing Catholic priests, Jesuits managed to care for Catholics in secret. Many of them died as martyrs, but there were always more men to replace them.

Because the Jesuits were so well educated, it was natural that they should become teachers themselves. Soon there were Jesuit colleges and universities throughout the world. In missionary territories, the first colleges were often Jesuit ones. By 1773, the Jesuits had established more than six hundred colleges and universities in Europe and the New World, as well as almost two hundred seminaries.

Protestants soon came to think of the Jesuits as the embodiment of all that was evil in the Church of Rome, and they became targets for violence and murder. But it was not only Protestants who were offended by Jesuits. In Catholic countries, the kings and princes often wanted more control over the Church than the pope was willing to give them. The Jesuits were like the pope's own private army, and their shrewd tactics thwarted the ambitions of some of the princes. Many rulers learned to hate the order because the Jesuits often acted as obstacles that prevented them from getting what they wanted.

The Flowering of Catholic Spain

In the 1500s, Spain was an enormous empire, the greatest power in Europe and one of the greatest the world had ever seen. Its American territories were expansive, and colonists sent home countless shiploads of gold every year. In Europe, Spanish monarchs ruled not only Spain itself but also the Netherlands and most of Italy. From north to south, Spain dominated the continent.

Even as Spain's worldly power reached its peak, the Church in Spain was blessed with some of the greatest mystics of all time. Many of those mystics faced serious opposition from Spanish clergymen and especially from the notorious Spanish Inquisition. With the memory of Muslim domination and persecution so fresh, it's not hard to understand why the Spanish were so eager to root out secret subversives. However, the Spanish Inquisition, headed by strong personalities, had spun out of control and had made life difficult for many sincere Christians. The Spanish mystics, in spite of the opposition they often faced, held firm to what they knew was right. Ultimately their light triumphed over the darkness.

One of these great mystics was St. Teresa of Avila, a Carmelite nun. In those days, religious life was not very strict. Nuns could own property outside the convent, receive visitors, and come and go at will. Teresa struggled with prayer in the distracting environment of the convent. One day in 1555, as she was praying in front of a borrowed statue of the wounded Christ, her heart broke as she realized how little she thanked Jesus for his suffering. From that day on her prayer life improved. She began to receive visions from God—"intellectual visions," as she called them, because instead of seeing sights, she felt knowledge impressed on her mind. Could God really be speaking to her, a sinner? Some of her friends told her that a demon must be supplying those visions. The Jesuit St. Francis Borgia saw the light of truth in Teresa, and he encouraged her to be open to what God was trying to tell her.

By 1558 Teresa had become convinced that the Carmelite order needed serious reforming. She advocated a return to the original rule of the Carmelites, which was one of the strictest of the monastic rules. The idea wasn't very popular among many of the Carmelites, and when Teresa established her first reformed convent in 1563, a riot nearly ensued. Nevertheless, Teresa found enough enthusiastic followers to make a flourishing community.

A few years later, in 1567, Teresa met another great Spanish mystic. Juan de Yepes y Álvarez, better known as St. John of the Cross, was a Carmelite friar, and he was also convinced that the Carmelites—men as well as women—needed reforming. By coincidence, Teresa had just received permission to establish two reformed monasteries for Carmelite friars. John joined her growing reform movement, and in a short time had created the first "Discalced" Carmelite monastery, so called because the inhabitants (like the original Carmelites) wore no shoes.

Both Teresa and John encountered fierce opposition among the Carmelites and interrogation by the Inquisition.

Teresa lived long enough to see her reforms vindicated. She died in 1582, worn out with the work of launching reformed Carmelite convents all over Spain. John of the Cross was even imprisoned for nine months. But it had always been his prayer "to suffer and be despised."[4] Eventually, even his enemies found they couldn't hate him. When he died in 1591, there was an outpouring of love and devotion that still continues today.

Teresa of Avila and John of the Cross lived in a century of crisis, but from that difficult century came astonishing developments in Catholic doctrine, spirituality, and culture—true reforms that are still appreciated and practiced in the Church today. ⹂

A Closer Look . . .

Erasmus, the Faithful Reformer

While Luther broke with the Church, many Christians did all they could to renew the Church from the inside.

Desiderius Erasmus was a scholar who believed that people could get along if they would just be reasonable with one another. His early career was much like Martin Luther's: like Luther, he became an Augustinian monk, and like Luther he found the Bible and the early Church Fathers much more satisfying than the works of the Scholastic philosophers. Like Luther, he was shocked by corruption in the hierarchy,

But Erasmus tried to reform the Church from the inside. He edited a famous edition of the New Testament in the original Greek, so that scholars could get as close as possible to what the Bible said. He wrote repeated pleas for reform and satires against the corruption he saw.

But while Luther broke from the Church, Erasmus stayed. The unity of the Church was more important to him than any reform. He worked hard to negotiate an agreement that would bring the Lutherans back without compromising any principles that were valid. He failed, and the war and bloodshed that he had feared happened anyway.

7

The Conversion of the New World

Christopher Columbus returned to Spain in 1493. He brought with him not only the colorful works of art he found in the New World but also some of the natives themselves. On Palm Sunday 1493, he marched with the natives in the annual procession in Seville. They were a sensation. No one could talk about anything else for weeks.

One eight-year-old boy watching that parade was so taken with the sight that he later ran off to the inn where the native people were staying to get a better look at them. His name was Bartolomé de Las Casas, and the experience would change the course of his life.

THE COLONIES

Pedro de Las Casas, the father of Bartolomé, was just as enthusiastic about the new discoveries as his young son. When he learned that Columbus was returning to the Indies, Pedro signed up for the next voyage. He would be one of a group of colonists who would venture to the New World in the hope of making a fortune and returning to Spain a wealthy man.

Five years later, Pedro did return to Spain wealthy. He also brought with him a gift for his teenage son: a native slave boy. The two boys became inseparable friends.

A few years later, Pedro returned to the Indies to stay, and when he was eighteen Bartolomé—who was studying for the priesthood—joined him on the island of Hispaniola. (Bartolomé would become the first priest to celebrate his ordination in the New World.) Columbus himself had given the family a farm there. Bartolomé made friends with many of the local people, and later noted:

> Once they begin to learn of the Christian faith they become so keen to know more, to receive the Sacraments, and to worship God, that the missionaries who instruct them do truly have to be men of exceptional patience and forbearance; and over the years I have time and again met Spanish laymen who have been so struck by the natural goodness that shines through these people that they frequently can be heard to exclaim: "These would be the most blessed people on earth if only they were given the chance to convert to Christianity."[1]

However, Bartolomé quickly found out that some of his Spanish countrymen were not so friendly with the natives. "The Spaniards have shown not the slightest consideration for these people," he wrote, "treating them (and I speak from first-hand experience, having been there from the outset) not as brute animals—indeed, I would to God they had done and had shown them the consideration they afford their animals—so much as piles of dung in the middle of the road."[2]

Many Spaniards came to the New World under the same arrangement that had first brought Pedro de Las Casas to the Indies. They were noblemen who would stay for five years and then go home, and during that time they expected to make as much money as possible. The best way to make money, of course, was not to work for it—such labor was beneath a nobleman—but to enslave the indigenous people and make them work for it. In Hispaniola and later in Cuba, Bartolomé de Las Casas would see firsthand how destructive these adventurers could be.

"It was upon these gentle lambs," he wrote, "imbued by the Creator with all the qualities we have mentioned, that from the very first day they clapped eyes on them the Spanish fell like ravening wolves upon the fold, or like tigers and savage lions who have not eaten meat for days. The pattern established at the outset has remained unchanged to this day, and the Spaniards still do nothing save tear the natives to shreds, murder them and inflict upon them untold misery, suffering and distress, tormenting, harrying and persecuting them mercilessly."[3]

The Voice of Christian Conscience

But the oppression did not go unnoticed or without protest. A group of Dominicans dared to speak out. In 1511, they chose Antón Montesino, well known as a fiery and eloquent preacher, to deliver a homily that would strike at the foundations of colonial power in the New World. On the second Sunday in Advent, he told the astonished congregation at the cathedral of Santo Domingo that anyone who held the natives as slaves could expect eternal damnation.

Bartolomé never forgot that homily. He himself had slaves, although he treated them kindly. But the Dominicans had planted doubts in his mind. Later, as he was reading the Old Testament Book of Sirach, he came upon this passage: "Like one who kills a son before his father's eyes is the person who offers a sacrifice from the property of the poor. The bread of the needy is the life of the poor; whoever deprives them of it is a murderer. To take away a neighbor's living is to commit murder; to deprive an employee of wages is to shed blood" (34:24-27).

The scales fell from Bartolomé's eyes. What was wrong was not only the cruelty of individual Spanish colonists but the whole system of enslaving the indigenous people who had a right to be free.

Las Casas would devote the rest of his life to defending the indigenous people. His greatest triumph was inspiring the 1537 papal bull *Sublimis Deus* ("The Sublime God"), in which Pope Paul III proclaimed that the indigenous tribes and any people who would be "discovered" in the future were equal before God.

New laws—spottily enforced, but still on the books—made the native people the subjects of the king of Spain, equal before the law to his Spanish subjects.

The Conquest of Mexico

The islands Columbus had discovered were inhabited by fairly primitive tribes. But from the beginning, the Spanish explorers heard rumors of magnificent cities filled with great stone buildings and practically littered with gold.

Amazingly enough, the rumors were true. In Mexico, and later in Peru, the Spanish found civilizations in many respects the equal of their own, and cities that surpassed anything they had ever seen in Europe.

It's a popular misconception that the Spanish viewed the civilized natives as primitive savages. When the Spanish explorers first encountered the Aztecs in 1519, they knew they had found a great civilization. "I could not possibly tell a hundredth of what could be said about these things," one of them wrote to King Philip of Spain. "But I will try to describe as well as I can what I have seen myself. And even though my attempt may not succeed perfectly, I know very well that what I have to tell will seem so wonderful that hardly anyone will believe it, since even those of us who have seen these things with our own eyes are still so amazed that we can't believe they're real."[4]

The writer was Hernán Cortés, and he was describing the great city of Temixtitlan (or Tenochtitlán), now Mexico City. In short, Cortés himself—the man responsible for conquering Mexico—saw immediately that he was in a civilized place. But the religion of the Aztec inhabitants regularly involved human sacrifices. It was a curious paradox: these obviously civilized people practiced a brutal and barbaric religion. According to one estimate, fifty thousand human victims were sacrificed to the Aztec gods every year. Based on reliable native chronicles, more than eighty thousand men had been sacrificed at once to dedicate a magnificent new temple in 1487, just a generation before the Spanish arrived.[5]

Cortés' description of some of the idols the Aztecs worshipped, which has been largely confirmed by archaeologists, explains why the Spanish found the native religion so horrific:

The figures of the idols in which these people believe surpass in stature a person of more than ordinary size; some of them are composed of a mass of seeds and leguminous plants, such as are used for food, ground and mixed together, and kneaded with the blood of human hearts taken from the breasts of living persons, from which a paste is formed in a sufficient quantity to form large statues. When these are completed they make them offerings of the hearts of other victims, which they sacrifice to them, and besmear their faces with the blood.[6]

Once Mexico had been conquered, the small number of Franciscan and Dominican missionaries living there faced an almost impossible task. The native people continued to live in fear of the bloodthirsty gods and resisted conversion.

OUR LADY OF GUADALUPE

In 1531—hardly a decade after the Spanish conquest—an enthusiastic convert, who had taken the Christian name Juan Diego, was hurrying down the hill to hear Mass in Mexico City. Suddenly the Blessed Virgin appeared to him. She gave him a message for the bishop: "Go to the palace of the bishop of Mexico. Tell him it is my great desire to have a temple built to me here. Tell him everything you've seen and heard. You can be sure that I will be very grateful and will reward you."

Bishop Zumárraga didn't believe Juan Diego at first. As he was returning home, the Blessed Virgin met him again.

"Obviously he thinks I made up my story," Juan Diego told her. "So I beg you, my Lady, send someone more worthy, someone well respected, so that they'll believe him. I'm nobody, just a little rope, the very end, a leaf."

"Listen, my dear little son," Mary replied, "I have many messengers I might send, but it is important that you yourself carry this message." She commanded him to go again to the bishop, and Juan Diego promised that he would.

The next day, Juan Diego carried out his promise, but the

bishop still didn't believe him. If anyone was going to believe his story, the bishop said, Juan Diego would need to have a sign from Our Lady—something that would prove that she really was the one who had appeared to him.

Juan Diego, a man of simple and trusting faith, believed that if he asked for a sign of the Blessed Virgin, she would surely give one to him. On his way back, he found her waiting for him again. She promised to meet him the next day and give him the sign he desired.

But Juan Diego didn't show up the next day. His elderly uncle—a man he dearly loved—had fallen ill. The doctors could not help him, and finally the uncle, who was also a Christian, asked Juan Diego to run for a priest so that he might make his confession and die in peace. Immediately Juan Diego set off for Mexico City. But what if he met the Blessed Virgin again? There was no time to waste even in talking to her. So he set out by a different route to to make sure he could avoid her. As he rounded a corner, to his surprise, there she was waiting for him.

"Where are you going?" she asked kindly.

With tears in his eyes, Juan Diego fell on his knees and told her all about his uncle. She told him not to worry: his uncle was cured. (And indeed he was, as Juan Diego later discovered.) Then she told him to climb the hill and gather the flowers he found there. Juan Diego was astounded to discover a patch of beautiful roses of all varieties, even though it was December, when no roses ought to be blooming at all. He gathered a huge bouquet of them in his *tilma*, a loose cloak that Mexicans wore. When he returned to Mary, she told him that the flowers were the sign he had asked for.

Carefully Juan Diego took the flowers, still wrapped in his

tilma, all the way to the bishop's palace. He told the bishop everything that had happened, adding that he had brought the sign. The flowers were amazing enough, and everyone in the palace remarked on them. But when Juan Diego let them fall out of his cloak, he was astonished to see the bishop and everyone else fall to their knees. There on his cloak was the image of the Virgin herself, just as he had described her.[7] And there it still is today, enshrined in the basilica of Guadalupe that was built at her command.

The effect of the apparition was immediate and profound. Until that time, the Christian faith had been imported by Spanish missionaries to the natives. Now, through this miraculous appearance, the Catholic faith would be homegrown, not only the religion of the Spanish but also a religion of the Mexicans.

Where all human means had failed, grace had succeeded. In just a few years, more than nine million Aztecs embraced the Catholic faith. The Mexican culture of death had withered at the touch of grace and died.

Juan Diego spent the rest of his life as a missionary, spreading the Catholic faith among the Mexican natives. He was devoted to the Eucharist, and by special dispensation of the bishop was allowed to receive Communion three times a week—a very unusual privilege in those days. Juan Diego was canonized in 2002 by Pope John Paul II.

The Reductions

In spite of Pope Paul III's most ardent efforts, Europeans in the New World continued to practice the slave trade. As Spanish slave hunters closed in on tribe after tribe in America, the desperate Franciscan and Jesuit missionaries came up with a way to save some of the tribes from total extermination. Beginning in 1609, with permission from the king of Spain, they formed Christian native villages called "reductions."

The reductions were scattered all over South and Central America, but the most famous ones were those established in Paraguay by the Jesuits. The colonists were opposed to the reductions because they protected the natives from slavery. But the reductions were welcome sanctuaries to the natives themselves. Whole tribes migrated hundreds of miles to live in the towns, where no slave hunter could enter. After a very short time, the reductions were healthy, tax-paying communities where the natives learned to read and write and run their own profitable farms. In fact, the natives were probably more literate than most of the European settlers outside the reductions. Many of the natives even learned to read Latin.

The reductions were an amazing success. Even people who weren't normally sympathetic to the Jesuits were impressed. Voltaire, the French philosopher of the Enlightenment who was critical of the Church, called the reductions "the triumph of humanity."[8]

This triumph did not last long, however. From the first, the Portuguese settlers in southern Brazil opposed the reductions, and periodically a band of raiders would descend on one of the peaceful villages and kidnap all the villagers so that they could be sold as slaves. Some of the Portuguese settlers were convinced that the Jesuits were secretly mining gold on their reductions, and they wanted that gold for themselves. Finally, in 1750, the Portuguese succeeded in convincing Spain to trade the lands on which the reductions were located in Paraguay for some other land, and immediately the new owners ordered the Jesuits and all the residents out.

The Jesuits did their best to lead their native friends peacefully to the far-off reservations set aside for them. But the people and their ancestors had lived in the reductions for more than a century, and now the Portuguese were heartlessly shipping them off to some unknown wasteland. Predictably, they rebelled, and even more predictably, they lost.

The enemies of the Jesuits in Portugal took advantage of this opportunity. Blaming the Jesuits for the rebellion, they persuaded the king to remove the Jesuits from his court. All the Jesuits were thrown out of Portugal's American colonies. This was only a glimpse of the future: the order was also under attack in other European countries from those who had long opposed it. In 1767, Jesuits were expelled from the Spanish possessions in America, and the reductions ended. Finally, in 1773, Pope Clement XIV bowed to the pressure from the European rulers and suppressed the Society of Jesus.

"Poor pope!" said St. Alphonsus Liguori. "What could he do in the circumstances in which he was placed, with all the sovereigns conspiring to demand this suppression? As for ourselves, we must keep silence, respect the secret judgment of God, and hold ourselves in peace."[9]

The suppression did not last long. The Society of Jesus was revived in 1814 by Pope Pius VII.

A Closer Look . . .

Pope St. Pius V

In spite of their attempts at reform, popes like Paul III still lived in obvious luxury. It was hard to persuade some bishops that they needed to reform when the popes themselves seemed to be living the good life. But in 1566, a pope was elected who embodied perfectly the new spirit of reform—so perfectly, in fact, that the Church remembers him as a saint, the first to sit on the throne of Peter for a long time. In the midst of the uncountable wealth of the Vatican, Pope Pius V lived a monk's life.

Pius V refused to have anything to do with the traditional practice of nepotism—that is, promoting one's family members to the highest levels of the Church. Instead, he promoted the best men regardless of their family connections. Not content with reforming the papacy and the Church, he reformed the city of Rome as well, which as pope he governed. Formerly notorious for its immorality, Rome appeared to have been transformed. There were strict punishments for adultery, profanity, and Sabbath breaking. The outward result was striking.

Some of the clergy resented the reforms of Pius V; they didn't like giving up their riches and their mistresses. But the pope applied every rule even more strictly to himself than he did to others. Even Protestants respected his morality, and in the Catholic Church the moral authority of the pope was much stronger.

8

The World Goes Mad

In 1776, a confederation of England's colonies in North America declared that they would no longer be ruled by their mother country. Instead of a king, they would institute a republican form of government. To the Europeans, this concept sounded like a bizarre fantasy. But after a long and bitter war, in which the French meddled considerably on the side of the colonies, England was forced to acknowledge America's independence.

Europeans were amazed by these events happening across the sea. The French especially, who were instrumental in the success of the American Revolution, were fascinated by men like Thomas Jefferson and Benjamin Franklin, who seemed to combine European refinement with colonial common sense. Inevitably, French intellectuals began to ask the obvious question: if it had worked in America, might it not also be possible for a European country to throw off tyranny and substitute liberty?

THE FRENCH REVOLUTION

Louis XIV, who ruled from 1643 until his death in 1715 and was known as the "Sun King," had made his country the glory of Europe but at the cost of ruining France economically. His successors would have to pay the price.

During the reign of his successor, King Louis XV, the poor were getting poorer—and in France the poor were the great majority. The oppressive tyranny of the monarchy was becoming unbearable, and French philosophers questioned its legitimacy: "I regard it then as certain," wrote the philosopher Jean-Jacques Rousseau, "that government did not begin with arbitrary power, but that this is the depravation, the extreme term, of government, and brings it back, finally, to just the law of the strongest, which it was originally designed to remedy."[1]

When King Louis XVI ascended the throne in 1774, it was a challenging time to be king in France, and he knew it. However, he was unable to implement any useful reforms, and conditions continued to deteriorate.

In 1789, King Louis, bankrupt and out of ideas, called a meeting of the Estates General, which was a French equivalent of Parliament or Congress. It hadn't met since 1614, so no one living had any practical experience with how it worked.

The body was supposed to be made up of three "estates": the nobles, the clergy, and the commoners. The first two estates each had three hundred members; the commoners had six hundred. But the relative numbers didn't matter, because each estate had only one vote. Any combination of two estates could outvote the third. Since the clergy almost always sided with the nobles, the commoners knew that they would always be outvoted.

Dissatisfied with such an arrangement, the commoners formed an assembly (the National Assembly) of their own and began to draft a new constitution for France. When the king tried to disband the assembly, mob violence broke out in Paris. On July 14, 1789, the mob stormed the Bastille, the city's notorious prison, and freed all the political prisoners there.

For a while the National Assembly ruled France as a constitutional monarchy, with Louis XVI forced to accept the role of figurehead. The king did not want to give up absolute power, however, so he conspired with his allies in Austria and Prussia

to reclaim it. Prussia issued a warning to the French revolutionaries not to harm the royal family. The National Assembly saw
this warning as evidence of the king's collusion, threw him in
prison, and went to war with Austria and Prussia. The French
revolutionary army defeated the Prussians, and on September
21, 1792, the new National Convention—which replaced the
assembly—declared an end to the monarchy.

A group in the National Convention that called themselves
the Girondists assumed leadership. They tried and executed the
former king for treason. In 1793, another group, calling themselves the Jacobins, gained power and executed the Girondists.
The Jacobins set up a "Committee of Public Safety" to rule the
country, and began to execute anyone even remotely suspected of
opposing them. For a year, the guillotines and other clever death
machines were kept busy. The Catholic Church was viewed as
an enemy, so the clergy suffered especially; anyone who admitted being faithful to the Church was killed. On the Ile Madame,
in the River Charente, almost one thousand priests were penned
up in a filthy prison camp and fed starvation rations. Hunger
and typhus killed 254 of them. For obvious reasons, history
calls this period "the Terror."

In 1794, the Jacobins' leader, Maximilien Robespierre, was
executed (it was his turn, after all), and the Terror ended.

Meanwhile, France had declared war on nearly every country
in Europe, and for a while it looked as though France might
conquer them all. Wherever the French conquered, they set up
puppet republican governments like their own.

In 1797, the brilliant general Napoléon Bonaparte conquered
most of Italy; and the following year, the French conquered
Rome itself, capturing the pope and setting up the usual puppet

republic. Napoléon, meanwhile, turned east and invaded Egypt and Syria.

It finally took an alliance of Austria, Britain, the kingdom of Naples, the Ottoman Empire, Portugal, and Russia to turn back the French tide in 1799.

Napoléon then went back to Paris and managed to overthrow the reigning government. He substituted a consulate, with himself as "first consul." In 1802, he was declared first consul for life, and in 1804, he scrapped the republic altogether and declared himself emperor of the French. The French Revolution was over.

From that short summary, it's apparent why the word "republican" meant something different in Europe from what it meant in the United States. In America of the 1800s, a republic was an orderly system of government based on ballots and constitutional law. To many European ears, the word "republic" meant terror, murder, mob violence, and anarchy. When we hear political leaders and even popes speaking out against republicanism, we have to remember that the example they had in mind was the French Revolution and the wars of conquest that followed it. As late as 1871, after another aborted revolution, the conservative newspaper *Le Figaro* in Paris suggested that the only good republican was a dead republican: "Today, clemency equals lunacy. What is a republican? A savage beast. We must track down those who are hiding, like wild animals. Without pity, without anger, simply with the steadfastness of an honest man doing his duty."

THE FRENCH REVOLUTION'S IMPACT ON THE CHURCH

Liberté, Égalité, Fraternité—"Liberty, Equality, Brother-hood"—was the slogan of the French Revolution, and those high ideals sound like Christian ones. But the revolutionaries saw the Church as the enemy, not as their ally. Almost immediately the National Assembly started tinkering with the structure of the Church in France. On July 12, 1790, almost exactly a year after the storming of the Bastille, the revolutionaries made the Church an arm of the state. The dioceses would be reorganized to conform to the new division of France into administrative departments, and the bishops and clergy would be elected by all citizens who were eligible to vote. The state would pay their wages. The pope would still be supreme in matters of doctrine, but he would have no authority in administrative matters.

The government required all the clergy to swear loyalty to the new constitution. Few of the bishops, and only a minority of the priests, would take the oath. (Some who did take the oath later recanted when they saw the direction the revolution was taking.) The result was a predictable schism in the French Church. The French seized Avignon, which until then had belonged to the popes, and during much of the revolution the state of France was openly at war with the Church. In 1792, rioters in Paris murdered every one of the dissident priests they could find—"a number of refractory Priests, all the Vicaires de Saint Sulpice, the directors of the Seminaries, and the Doctors of the Sorbonne, with the *ci-devant* Archbishop of Arles, and a number of others, exceeding in all one hundred and seventy,"[2] according to an English diplomat who observed the events.

During the Terror, the clergy who remained faithful to the Church were in constant danger of their lives. They traveled in disguise; they hid in the homes of faithful friends; and many of them died on the guillotine rather than deny the Church. As it turned out, the clergy who sided with the new Constitutional Church hardly fared better. By this time, the revolution had gone far beyond the idea of nationalizing the Church. Now the revolutionaries aimed at nothing less than creating an entirely new religion.

It was difficult for the revolutionaries to agree, however, on what that religion should be. At one point they attempted to introduce the worship of Reason as a goddess. "Legislators!" one of them proclaimed, introducing the new religion to the assembly. "Fanaticism has given way to reason. Its bleared eyes could not endure the brilliancy of the light. This day an immense concourse has assembled beneath those gothic vaults, which, for the first time, re-echoed the truth." (He was talking about the Cathedral of Notre-Dame, which the revolutionaries had renamed the Temple of Reason.) "There the French have celebrated the only true worship—that of Liberty, that of Reason. There we have formed wishes for the prosperity of the arms of the Republic. There we have abandoned inanimate idols for Reason, for that animated image, the masterpiece of nature."

Then the goddess of Reason herself was brought out, and the same legislator announced: "Mortals, cease to tremble before the powerless thunders of a God whom your fears have created. Henceforth acknowledge no divinity but Reason. I offer you its noblest and purest image; if you must have idols, sacrifice only to such as this."[3]

The "noblest and purest image" of Reason was a popular

dancer from the Paris stage, dressed in a classical costume. She was led with great pomp to the Cathedral of Notre-Dame, where a stage setting from Greek mythology had been prepared for her. With impressive ceremony, the actress was plunked down on the altar. Then the legislators threw a wild party in the cathedral that lasted far into the night.

The notorious Robespierre, who came into power a short time later, was a deist and proclaimed that atheism was dangerous to the state. He attempted to establish his own deist religion, but it didn't have any time to take root before Robespierre himself was executed.

A movement known as Theophilanthropism represented the revolutionaries' final attempt to establish a new religion. Based on the principles of goodness and, of course, loyalty to the state, it spread to some of the great churches of France, including the much-abused Cathedral of Notre-Dame. Although it failed to win any lasting popular support, it was the most persistent of the new religions. For a hundred years, whenever republican ideas were fashionable again in France, someone would attempt to revive Theophilanthropism and preach it to the masses.

All these new religions failed not only because they were false, but, more important, because the hearts of the French people were still with the Catholic Church. When Napoléon restored peace to France, the Church—in spite of a decade of persecution as savage as Diocletian's—was still there, still doing its work. In 1801, Napoléon signed a *concordat* or agreement acknowledging that the Roman Catholic Church was the religion of "the great majority of the French," and the French Church was back in business. Napoléon didn't stick to the agreement very well, but at least the clergy no longer feared for their lives.

In 1804, when Napoléon decided to have himself crowned emperor of the French, he invited Pope Pius VII to crown him at Paris. Against the advice of the Curia, Pope Pius accepted the invitation, hoping he could put Napoléon in a friendlier mood toward the Church. It didn't work. Napoléon was determined to have his own way in everything, whatever the pope thought of it.

KIDNAPPING THE POPE

In 1808, Napoléon tired of the pope's stubborn refusal to annul his brother's legal marriage, close his ports to Napoléon's enemies, and recognize all Napoléon's puppet rulers in Europe. He invaded Rome. The next year, he declared that the papal states were permanently annexed to the French Empire. Pope Pius responded by excommunicating Napoléon and everyone else who had been responsible for the annexation.

"What does the Pope mean by the threat of excommunicating me?" the emperor demanded. "Does he think the world has gone back a thousand years? Does he suppose the arms will fall from the hands of my soldiers?"[4] On July 5, 1809, Napoléon arrested Pius, and until the end of his empire, he held the pope hostage, shuffling him around from town to town and forcing the pontiff to sign agreements giving Napoléon more control of the French Church. Pope Pius repudiated the agreements he had signed under duress, refusing to be bullied into giving Napoléon the control he wanted.

THE CURÉ OF ARS

The stubbornness of the pope would have meant nothing without the faith of millions of ordinary Christians. One whose simple faith influenced thousands was St. John Vianney.

Vianney couldn't pass the entrance exams for the seminary the first time he took them. He couldn't follow classes in Latin. He was last in a class of two hundred at his seminary. When he finally was ordained a priest, his superiors sent him to a backwater country parish in the village known as Ars where he wouldn't be in the way.

But Jean-Baptiste-Marie Vianney became the best-known parish priest of his time. Today we know him as St. John Vianney, the *curé* (parish priest) of Ars, the patron of priests throughout the world.

It was a tough time to be a priest. When young Jean-Baptiste was growing up, the revolutionary government in France had outlawed the Catholic religion. By the time he became a priest, many of the people had forgotten or never known the Christian faith.

Living a life of constant prayer and fasting, the new priest gave up almost every one of his possessions to the poor. Then he preached a simple message of repentance, urging his parishioners to give up pleasure-seeking and turn back to God. A priest could preach no other message, he said. "Even if he knew he would be killed when he got down from the pulpit, he couldn't let that stop him."[5]

But Vianney's parishioners didn't kill him. Instead, they listened. And, moved by his pious example, they began to practice what he preached. Soon word spread about the exceptionally holy curé of Ars whose simple words moved full-grown men to weep.

From all over France, people flocked to Ars to hear Vianney preach or to make their confession to him. Whenever the cynics complained that the curé wasn't well enough educated to be preaching or hearing confessions, his own bishop silenced them. "I don't know whether he's educated or not," the bishop said, "but I do know that the Holy Spirit makes a point of enlightening him."[6]

By 1855 hundreds of pilgrims were coming to Ars. The railroad had to build a new station there just to handle the traffic. Hotels opened in the village, and the fields were full of camping pilgrims. The holy curé was spending eighteen hours a day in the confessional. He also became known for miraculous healings—miracles that continued after his death. John Vianney was canonized in 1925.

THE CHURCH RESTORED—FOR A WHILE

In 1814, Napoléon's empire fell apart, and Pope Pius VII went back to Rome. The papal states were restored, and Pope Pius was now the hero of the resistance to Napoléon. The rest of his life was devoted to restoring the Church in Europe. He reinstituted the Jesuit order, and he worked hard to come to diplomatic agreements with Prussia, Bavaria, and Russia.

More important, there were signs of an authentic revival in the Church, even in France. Young people, including young intellectuals, were returning to the Christian faith. In the years that followed, the Catholic Church slowly gained back some of its old rights and privileges in Europe. In England, the Catholic Emancipation Act of 1829 ended the persecution of Catholics.

In Ireland, where the Catholic population had long been forced to support the Protestant Church of England, the priests were allowed to do their work without being bothered. The Irish still had to pay for the support of the empty Protestant churches, but at least they were at liberty now to declare proudly that they were Catholics.

RISE OF THE KNOW-NOTHINGS

It was not only in Europe that the Church had troubles. The United States of America was founded on principles of liberty for all, and religious liberty was one of the country's most prized traditions. But it was also a country where the great majority of the ruling class was Protestant; only one Catholic—Charles Carroll—had been among those who signed the Declaration of Independence.

Most of those Protestants were fiercely dedicated to the ideal of religious liberty for all. But a noisy minority found it impossible to extend the idea of religious liberty to Catholics. At first their numbers were small. But as more and more Catholic immigrants came into the country, anti-Catholic bigotry grew from a nuisance to an epidemic. Prejudice was now supplemented by violence. The fanatics were still a small minority compared to the great majority of peaceful citizens, but they were a dangerous minority who didn't care that they were condemned by Catholics and law-abiding Protestants alike.

By the 1840s, a loose coalition of secret terrorist societies was beginning to make their presence known. They were a motley assortment, harboring a variety of prejudices, but they had in common their bitter hatred of anything Catholic. They met in secret to plan attacks against Catholics and their property, and—like all terrorist fanatics—they were firmly convinced of the nobility of their cause. Their favorite sport was arson.

One Catholic newspaper wrote in 1844,

Within the last few years, our enemies have banded themselves together, and what bounds have they placed on their denunciations? We have been represented as enemies of God, and traitors to our country. The foulest crimes which God denounced in His sacred oracles are stated to be our most cherished dogmas. We are held up to the world as meditating designs systematically destructive of our political institutions. We are accused of making religion a veil for the most foul corruption and an engine of the most deadly treachery. Our private morals are attacked, the most vile insinuations are made against the most consistent and virtuous amongst us. We are accused of crimes which if brought home in detail to any individual would make him an outcast from society, and consign him—and justly, too—to the severest penalties of the law."[7]

One of the more explosive episodes occurred in Philadelphia and involved the King James Bible. In the public schools, the King James version, an English translation of Scripture first published by Protestants in 1611, was read to the children every day. Bishop Francis Kenrick of Philadelphia asked that the Catholic children be allowed to have the Douay Version, the translation of the Latin Vulgate Bible approved by the Catholic Church, read to them instead.

Immediately there were charges that the Catholics were trying to take the Bible out of the schools, and that their own version of the Bible was a perversion of the one true translation, the King James Version. After a meeting on May 6, 1844, the most fanatical elements in the crowd rushed out to burn down the shanties and hovels of the Irish Catholic immigrants. The next night they first set fire to the fire station in the Irish neighborhood, and then burned down more houses. Neighboring Protestant firefighters just sat and watched the glow.

On May 8, the mob turned up at St. Michael's Church. The captain of the militia—the police force that was supposed to be keeping order—demanded the keys to the church from the priest. Then he had his men stand by and watch while the mob burned the church and the rectory.

Of course, these extremists were only a tiny minority of the Protestants in the city. When the Protestant mayor, John Morin Scott, heard that St. Augustine's Church was next on the list to be burned, he heroically led the city watch to protect the building and stood guard with them himself. The mob came and beat him senseless, scattered the watchmen, and burned the church. Then they went off and burned a convent.

It wasn't until May 10 that the authorities finally put a stop to the riots. By that time, dozens of buildings were in smoldering ruins, and a number of innocent Irish citizens had been murdered. But no one was convicted of any crimes.

Two months later, in July, some of the same rioters found a cannon and rolled it up to St. Philip Neri's Church. There was a pitched battle between the rioters and the militia, and several people were killed.

New York suffered from anti-Catholic mobs as well. Bishop John Hughes was ready. He arranged for each church to be defended by an army of more than a thousand well-armed parishioners. Their instructions: to die fighting if that was necessary.

"Are you afraid that some of your churches will be burned?" the mayor asked Bishop Hughes when the bishop told him of his plans.

"No, sir," the bishop replied, "but I am afraid some of yours will be burned. We can protect our own. I come to warn you for your own good."[8]

The bishop's quick reaction saved the churches of New York. He also wrote and published a letter to the mayor challenging anyone—especially the editors of the anti-Catholic papers—to show that he had ever been a disloyal citizen of the United States. "I have never in my life done one action, or uttered a sentiment tending to abridge any human being of all or any of the rights of conscience which I claim to enjoy myself under the American constitution," he wrote.[9] Hundreds of thousands of people read the letter the day it was published, and all but the most fanatical Protestants were convinced. In spite of threats against his life, Bishop Hughes managed to keep New York peaceful.

But as the tens of thousands of Irish immigrants poured into every corner of the United States, the anti-Catholic prejudice spread. It began to infect politics. In Pittsburgh, a vulgar anti-Catholic street preacher named Joe Barker was elected mayor; his first act was to have the bishop of Pittsburgh arrested on trumped-up charges. As mayor, he continued his favorite sport of spending Sunday afternoons under the windows of the Catholic seminary, shouting insults at the students. But his buffoonery annoyed even his supporters, and within a year he was convicted of various crimes while in office.

Sometimes mobs gathered and burned Catholic churches; at

other times, Catholic churches simply caught fire under mysterious circumstances. Some new Catholic churches were built without ground-floor windows, since the mobs would certainly smash any windows within reach. Others sprouted defensive walls, like medieval monasteries expecting Viking raids.

From Maine to Texas, there were reports of rioters killing priests and destroying Catholic property. In Massachusetts and in Ohio, churches were blown to bits with gunpowder. The Bloody Monday riot of 1855 in Louisville left twenty-five Irish Catholics dead and the cathedral in ashes. In 1851, rioters in Washington, DC, seized a block of marble and dumped it into the Potomac; Pope Pius IX had donated the stone for the Washington Monument.

One of the favorite techniques of the rioters was to gather along the streets when they knew Catholic schoolchildren or women on their way to Mass would be passing by. When the Catholics came in view, the mob would erupt with a volley of obscene insults. If the insults didn't hurt enough, the rioters would throw stones. The idea was to get the Catholic men so furious at seeing their children, wives, and mothers subjected to such treatment that they would finally attack the taunting mob. Then the Protestants would have to defend themselves, of course, reporting to often-sympathetic authorities that the Catholics were starting riots.

It was all the bishops could do sometimes to keep the peace. Bishop O'Connor of Pittsburgh promised to lead the people himself if it became necessary to defend their churches. "Stir neither hand nor foot," he said, "but if they attempt to fire your asylum or your church, I will head you."[10]

In 1852, the various secret societies organized themselves

into one political party, officially called the National Council of the United States of North America. Every new member took an oath never to reveal any of the secrets of the organization. So the rest of the country called them Know-Nothings, because if they were asked a question about their party they would always reply, "I don't know."

It was a hard time for Catholics in America. But their patient endurance, courage, charity, and reasoned behavior prepared the way for their descendants, a century later, to play an influential role in the nation and the culture. 🐉

A Closer Look . . .

The Steam-Bishop of Charleston

Charleston, the grand old city in South Carolina, was the cultural capital of the South, so it was natural that it should be the seat of the South's first Catholic bishop. In 1821, an Irish bishop, ironically named John England, came to preside over the new See of Charleston. It was a huge, sprawling diocese, covering both North and South Carolina and Georgia.

Charleston itself was already a century and a half old and set in its ways. Many of its earliest settlers had been French Huguenots fleeing the religious wars in Europe. Even as late as 1775, Catholics were tarred and feathered there for no other crime than being Catholic. But with the American Revolution came religious tolerance, grudgingly but legally enforced. Most of the South was belligerently anti-Catholic, but at least there was no law against the Catholic Church, and there were small groups of Catholics here and there, who were mostly Irish immigrants.

First Bishop England surveyed the situation. What he found was hardly an excuse for a diocese. There were only two Catholic churches open in all three states, each with one priest. That was the extent of the Church's presence in the South.

England got to work. He traveled everywhere in his diocese, often on foot. He walked so much, in fact, that he wore out the soles of his shoes. Wherever he found a little group of Catholics, he organized them and helped them stay together until he could send them a priest.

In the small southern towns there wasn't much in the way of entertainment, and a Catholic bishop in full regalia wasn't something you saw every day. So when Bishop England came to town everyone—Protestant and Catholic alike—came out to take a look. When they heard him preach, they stayed.

That's because Bishop England was a spellbinding preacher. And the Protestants who flocked to hear him in increasing numbers were amazed to hear what sounded like good Christian doctrine in his sermons. Not long after his arrival, he established a reputation as one of the best preachers in the South. Soon he was invited to preach in public buildings wherever he went. Even Protestant churches would invite him to preach. When he was in Charleston, his preaching was a regular spectacle, attracting huge crowds.

Often his subject was "the nature of the Catholic religion," about which most of the Protestants in the South knew almost nothing. He was often able to convince at least some in the crowd that Catholics were actually Christian after all.

Preaching wasn't the only way to reach people, of course. Bishop England also made successful ventures into publishing, and he founded a school to give the young people of Charleston a classical education. He launched an organization that opposed dueling, a practice that was still a problem in the South. He was even invited to speak to the US House of Representatives, the first Catholic clergyman ever to set foot in those halls. At the Vatican, he was known as the Steam-Bishop of America, because he seemed to keep going and going like an unstoppable machine.

But Bishop England wasn't unstoppable. When an epidemic hit, England's sense of Christian charity compelled him to minister to the sick. He traveled to Europe in 1842, and on the way back, dysentery broke out in steerage—the lower levels of the ship, in the wretched accommodations of the poorest classes. He spent the whole voyage ministering to the sick, and in the end he caught the disease himself. When the ship landed in Philadelphia, in spite of the disease, he immediately resumed his hectic preaching schedule. But at last, the infection got the better of him. He died begging his friends' forgiveness for not always having been charitable enough, but there probably wasn't an American Catholic alive who would have made that accusation against Bishop England.

9

The Secular Age

The Church was now entering the most dangerous era in her history—a time when some even inside the Church questioned whether the institution would survive. By the mid-nineteenth century, all the forces that had been gathering against the Church in the previous centuries—Protestantism, revolutionary philosophy, nationalism, and industrial regimentation—were combining to attack it. The pope had been deprived of his temporal power and was shut up in the Vatican. All over Europe, anticlerical governments were taking away the Church's property and putting severe restrictions on priests.

Yet the Church would come out of the fire refined and stronger. As Christ had promised, the gates of hell would not prevail against it.

INTELLECTUAL DISCONTENT

After decades of persecution by political ideologies, it's not surprising that some influential people within the Church grew suspicious of all intellectual undertakings. Some churchmen reacted so strongly to the wayward philosophies of the past that they discouraged any serious study of philosophy at all. In the average French seminary, for example, students heard quite a few lectures on the evils of the French Revolution and Voltaire but seldom or never read any of the works of the great Catholic thinkers of the past. Instead, they were required to memorize long lists of propositions that simply restated the doctrines of the Church without explaining how or why the Church had arrived at them. Even Scripture was reduced to a dry textbook.

It's hardly surprising, then, that some Catholics—with no intellectual guidance—went down the wrong paths. Since they had heard no philosophical defense of some of the Church's doctrines, these "Modernists" jumped to the conclusion that those doctrines were indefensible. And if they were indefensible, then they ought to be thrown out. The pope, they believed, ought to come to terms with progress and secularism. In an 1864 "Syllabus of Errors," Pope Pius IX condemned many of the modern ideas in the movements gaining currency at the time, such as rationalism and communism. To the Modernists, the pope's encyclical just proved that he was part of the problem.

In fact, some intellectuals confidently predicted the end of the papacy itself. The pope was a relic of the Middle Ages, they said. His temporal authority in Italy had already come to an end; he would soon have to admit that his spiritual authority was ending as well.

But Pope Pius IX was certainly not ready to give up. He knew what his opponents neglected to consider: that the huge masses of faithful ordinary believers were on his side. In fact, they positively loved him. Pius IX was the first really popular pope in history, the first one who became a hero in magazines and newspapers. Millions of ordinary believers were loyal to him, not just as pope but as a real person. They loved him, and they knew that he loved them.

Still, there were plenty of reasons to believe that the papacy was in serious trouble. Pius IX was a prisoner in the Vatican. In Italy, anticlerical mobs sometimes beat up believers on their way to Mass. The situation was even worse in Spain and France, where priests legitimately feared for their lives. In Germany, the ruthless and relentless Prussian government would soon declare open war on the Church. And finally, there were the Modernists inside the Church, calling for a new brand of Christianity in which no one would insist on belief in what they considered to be outdated superstitions that acted as stumbling blocks to the wise.

Meanwhile, other enemies were attacking Rome with guns instead of ideas.

The End of the Papal Dominions

Since the Dark Ages, the popes had governed Rome and the areas of Italy surrounding it. But in the 1800s, the whole peninsula of Italy had gradually been united, and the pope was left with nothing but Rome itself.

In 1870, the Franco-Prussian War broke out, and all Europe was distracted. It was a perfect time for King Victor Emmanuel of Italy to fulfill his last ambition: to make Rome his capital. He marched his army into the city and took over, installing himself in the papal palace of the Quirinal. Rome now belonged to Italy, not to the pope. Pope Pius IX, naturally, was furious, but there was no one to come to his aid. The rest of Europe was either at war or enjoying the spectacle of Prussia beating up France. The unprovoked seizure of Rome was hardly noticed.

By the Law of Guarantees in 1871, the Italian government allowed the pope to keep the Vatican and Lateran palaces, as well as his summer retreat at Castel Gandolfo. But Pope Pius IX shut himself up in the Vatican and refused to come out. He also prohibited Catholics from participating in the Italian government.

For the next fifty years, Italian Catholics would feel the tension between loyalty to their state and loyalty to their Church.

However, in the end, the loss of temporal power was probably a blessing for the popes and the Church. Italian politics could often distract a pope from his duties to the universal Church. And the mere fact that he was lord of a temporal government, with all the corruption, inefficiency, and imperfection that went with it, sometimes muddied the pope's moral authority. With no local government to run, the popes could put all their resources into their spiritual leadership.

As for the Vatican Council that had been convened in 1869 during Pius IX's papacy, the invasion cut it off in the middle and scattered the assembled prelates. They never got back together, and the council was never officially adjourned.

THE CULTURE WAR

In Germany, the history of the 1800s is mostly a history of how the land finally became a unified nation. More pessimistically, we might say that it's primarily a history of how the brutal and efficient Prussian state conquered the colorful assortment of German principalities and tried to make them all Prussian. Most of that conquest was the work of Otto von Bismarck, the pragmatic and capable minister whose one ambition was to restore the great German Empire.

In 1870, the French emperor Napoléon III decided to stop Prussia in its tracks. But he was defeated so soundly in the resulting Franco-Prussian War that France had to surrender two provinces, the French Empire fell apart, and a Communist government took over briefly in Paris. Prussia, on the other hand, was now the leading power of continental Europe, and in 1871 a new German Empire was declared, with Wilhelm I, the king of Prussia, as the new caesar (*kaiser* in German).

With this string of successes, Otto von Bismarck, the minister, decided to consolidate the German Empire's power by eliminating all hostile "non-German" influences. At the top of the list was the Catholic Church, headed by a pope who wasn't even German. The German government seized Catholic schools, deported the Jesuits and several other religious orders, and took over the seminaries. Bishops and other clergymen who protested were thrown in prison. It was nothing less than a war against the Church—a war Bismarck called a culture war, or *Kulturkampf* in German.

With all his skill, however, Bismarck couldn't win this war. Instead of consolidating Prussia's power over Germany, the Kulturkampf mobilized Catholics, rousing them with a renewed zeal and enthusiasm for their faith. A new Catholic political party rapidly gained ground. When Leo XIII, the newly elected pope, offered Bismarck a few face-saving concessions, Bismarck realized he had been beaten, and one by one, the repressive laws against Catholics were repealed. By 1887, the Church had won the culture war, not by force of arms but through the loyalty of millions of ordinary Catholics.

Things to Come

On October 13, 1884, Pope Leo XIII had a vision in which Satan vowed to destroy the Church in the twentieth century.[1]

Leo was convinced that the vision was a true prophecy of terrible things to come. The Church, he decided, must mobilize to fight the forces of darkness. Among other things, he added the prayer to St. Michael the Archangel to the end of the Mass:

> St. Michael the Archangel, defend us in battle!
> Be our protection against the wickedness and snares
>   of the devil.
> May God rebuke him, we humbly pray,
>   and do thou, O Prince of the heavenly host,
>   by the power given you by God,
>   thrust into hell Satan and all the other evil spirits
>   who roam about the world seeking the ruin of souls.

The prayer was still used at the end of the Mass until the late 1960s, and Pope John Paul II strongly encouraged Catholics to pray it privately and publicly.

But while the Church gathered all its resources to prepare for the cataclysms to come, one young cloistered nun had already shown the modern world a simpler cure for its ills.

A MODERN SAINT

No other saint influenced twentieth-century spirituality as profoundly as Thérèse Martin. Her Little Way—both directly, through its adherents, and indirectly, through its influence—has shown itself grand enough to accommodate millions of modern people.

Who was Thérèse, that she should become the quintessential "modern" saint? She's often described by what she was not. She was not extraordinarily intelligent. She wasn't especially sweet tempered. She received little in the way of extraordinary mystical gifts—no visions, voices, or visitations. In her earthly days, she worked no miracles. She practiced nothing but the modest fasts and mortifications that were customary for her state of life.

Thérèse lived a short life—only twenty-four years—and nine of those years were passed in the obscurity of a Carmelite cloister. She prayed; and she labored, like all of us, at laundry and housework and other mundane tasks. When she died in 1897 of tuberculosis, she left behind little more than a small bundle of notebooks. Judging only by productivity, one might be tempted to agree with one nun who lived with Thérèse and who summed her up as "good for nothing."[2] Thérèse, too, might agree. Her way to holiness was a way so hidden, so modest—so "little"— that hardly anyone noticed.

Although the western world boasted its "coming of age"—with its great strides in science, technology, and industry—Thérèse chose to heed Jesus' words in Matthew's gospel: "Unless you change and become like children, you will never enter the kingdom of heaven" (Matthew 18:3). She strove to become ever more childlike in her love of God. Her Little Way might be summed up in this way: the love of God and others is the primary vocation of every Christian; we need to rely on God to become holy as a child would rely on her parents; and we can use the ordinary circumstances of everyday life as opportunities to offer God our love.

These ran counter to the spiritual currents of her day. In fact, Thérèse seems to have sketched out her Little Way at least partly in response to her older sister Céline, also a Carmelite, who was bent on working out her salvation through heroic mortification, intense study, and hard work. Thérèse wrote, "We are living now in an age of inventions, and we no longer have to take the trouble of climbing stairs, for in the homes of the rich, an elevator has replaced these very successfully. I wanted to find an elevator which would raise me to Jesus, for I am too small to climb the rough stairway to perfection."[3]

Those notebooks Thérèse left, compiled as *Story of a Soul*, first rolled off the presses in 1898. By the time she was canonized in 1925, her book had been translated into more than forty languages, selling many millions of copies, with immediate and lasting effect. Looking back, we can see Thérèse's profound influence on many of the spiritual movements of our century.

Dorothy Day, founder of the Catholic Worker movement, was at first repulsed by the saccharine piety Catholics professed for "Little Thérèse"—portrayed on Day's first Catholic prayer book as "a young nun with a sweet insipid face, holding a crucifix and a huge bouquet of roses." When Day first read *Story of a Soul*, she "found it colorless, monotonous, too small in fact for my notice."

Yet, over time, Day would come to see Thérèse's insignificance as the saint's most significant quality. In 1960, Day—who spent her life serving the poor—wrote *Thérèse*, a book-length study of the saint. Day wrote the book, she explained, "to overcome the sense of futility in Catholics, men, women, and youths, married and single, who feel hopeless and useless, less than the dust, ineffectual, wasted, powerless." Thérèse, like us, was all these things, yet she "was little less than the angels," Day wrote. "And so are we all."[4]

Day's contemporary, Catherine Doherty, the founder of Madonna House, taught a deep spirituality of simplicity and service. Evoking Thérèse for her own followers, Doherty wrote,

I think of people who work day in, day out, doing little things. Let's say you are in your kitchen, peeling potatoes with great love for God, in your duty of the moment. I see you there, and suddenly, with the eyes of my soul, I see the very peelings are transformed into threads of silver and gold, stretched up to heaven as hosannas to glorify God! To some people God gives great graces. . . . But you may have a hidden life, a life of small things through which you can come to God in a little way, like the Little Flower St. Thérèse did.[5]

As if in confirmation of Thérèse's Little Way, the causes for canonization of both Day and Doherty have been introduced in recent years.

Another modern saint, Josemaría Escrivá de Balaguer, founded Opus Dei in Spain in 1928, only three years after Thérèse was canonized. Through the founding years of Opus Dei, he would use *Story of a Soul* as spiritual reading for the organization's first members. In his own seminal work, *The Way*, St. Josemaría echoed Thérèse's Little Way in chapters titled "Little Things," "Life of Childhood," and "Spiritual Childhood." In one point for meditation, Escrivá seems to hold up Thérèse as a measure for the Christian's exceeding love for Christ: "Be daring: tell Him you are more carried away with love than . . . little Thérèse."[6]

What is amazing is that someone "little" as Thérèse could bear so many "big" titles: model for souls, copatron of the missions, copatroness of France, and even doctor of the Church. But the millions of Christians who know Thérèse Martin through her writings prefer to call her "the Little Flower."

A Closer Look . . .

A Saint Who Knew How to Bluff

In 1844, St. Philomena's was a poor German parish in Pittsburgh that had begun a magnificent Gothic building, but no one knew where the money would come from to finish it. Fr. John Neumann, the first Redemptorist to make his profession in America, had a bustling congregation but only half a building.

Like many other priests facing that sort of problem, Fr. Neumann ended up becoming something of a financial wizard. His friend and colleague Fr. Francis Seelos, also a priest at St. Philomena's, remembered that money was always short. "Often on a Friday he never knew where he was going to get the money for the payroll on Saturday."

Fr. Neumann sometimes resorted to bluff when there was no alternative. One tradition tells of the time a creditor, convinced that the parish was nearly bankrupt, stormed into the rectory and demanded his money immediately. Fr. Neumann calmly asked whether he desired to be paid in silver or in gold; and the reassured creditor, certain that his money was in safe hands if the pastor could offer him that choice, withdrew his demand and went on his way. Of course, Fr. Neumann had neither silver nor gold to give him. But somehow, the church was completed in 1846, causing Bishop O'Connor of Pittsburgh to remark that Fr. Neumann had managed to build a church without money.

Fr. Neumann left Pittsburgh shortly after that. Though he was still a young man, his health was declining, and his doctor advised a change of climate. But in less than a month, he was appointed superior of the Redemptorists in America—a position that required even more hard work. Later he became bishop of Philadelphia, where he continued to wear himself down with charitable work. He died in 1860 at the age of forty-eight. But his flock kept alive the memory of his exceptional piety and charity. In 1977, he was canonized, and now the body of St. John Neumann lies under the altar of St. Peter's Church in Philadelphia.

Perhaps the most remarkable tribute to his influence is the fact that his friend and successor at St. Philomena's, Fr. Seelos, also lived a life of such exemplary faith that he was beatified by Pope John Paul II. Blessed Francis Seelos followed his mentor's example.

10

A Century of Cataclysms

The twentieth century would live up to Pope Leo's dire vision. The First World War was a cataclysm like nothing the world had ever seen before, one that destroyed an entire generation of Europe's young men and left the whole continent in ruins. Yet, in many ways it was just the prelude to the greater cataclysm to come.

MUSSOLINI

Benito Mussolini might have ended up a harmless buffoon if he hadn't become so powerful. As a child, he was thrown out of boarding school and his mother's church for his behavior. He emigrated to Switzerland to avoid military service but was deported back to Italy. He also wrote several novels and intended to write a complete history of religion, but he never got further than one particularly nasty essay about the Bohemian rebel Jan Huss.

In those early years, Mussolini had been a Socialist. But during World War I, he turned against all his former principles and allied himself with what he used to call the bourgeoisie—the middle classes, who lived in fear of a workers' revolt that would turn Italy Communist. His new Fascist Party (from the *fasces*, the ancient Roman symbol of authority) stood for "law and order," which in practice meant killing anyone who rebelled against Mussolini's authority. Rapidly rising in power, Mussolini felt secure enough by 1922 to march on Rome with his army of devoted "black shirts" and take complete control of the country.

For the first few years, *Il Duce* ("the Leader," as Mussolini was known) had widespread popular support. Chaos had gripped Italy before Mussolini came to power; now he took credit for making the trains run on time. The economy was good, the Communists were crushed, and order was restored, so the people overlooked the brutality of the Fascist gangs and the fact that some of the workers might be underpaid and malnourished.

Although Mussolini was hardly a Christian himself, he needed the support of the Church to make his regime seem legitimate. In 1929, therefore, he reached an agreement with Pope Pius XI that ended the half century of antagonism between the Vatican and the Italian government. The Lateran Treaty created Vatican City, a tiny but independent state ruled by the pope. Castel Gandolfo and some other tracts of land were also made "extra-territorial" properties of the Vatican. The treaty also made the Catholic Church the only legal religion of Italy, and it gave the pope millions of lire in compensation for the loss of the papal states. Pope Pius XI was amazed by Mussolini's generosity; he declared that the man had been sent by divine providence. He would live to regret that ill-considered statement.

But for the time being, Mussolini's government was the model of success. Fascist parties of various sorts sprouted in every European country.

What was Fascism? Simply put, it was the doctrine that the state is all-important. Freedom and individual rights have no meaning, because the individual is to be judged only by his usefulness to the state. Representative democracy was repudiated, because, the Fascists said, it was inefficient and mediocre. Instead, under Fascism, by the will of the people one heroic dictator is chosen who has absolute power to make all decisions.

In practice, Mussolini and his imitators gained power by appealing to the poorer classes and kept their power by sharing it with giant corporations. Mussolini stayed in power because his Fascist government brought order. It was a brutal order, but it seemed better than chaos.

Hitler the Moral Reformer

Of all the European nations at this time, Germany was in the most difficult straits. The Allies had blamed Germany for the World War, and the reparations they forced Germany to pay were ruinous. German money was worthless, and millions of Germans were out of work. The threat of a Communist take-over was real. It was no surprise, then, that Germany ended up producing its own homegrown Fascist.

The situation was dire in Germany when Hitler came to power, and in a relatively short time it improved. That was what made him popular at first. After he had a solid grip on power, Hitler could rule by terror and didn't have to be concerned about his popularity.

As for his politics, Hitler borrowed some of Mussolini's ideas. Like Mussolini, Hitler threw out traditional democracy and sub-stituted the rule of the heroic dictator—namely, himself. But Hit-ler added a few poisonous ideas of his own. For him, the German "race"—not the nation—was all important, and its survival was imperative. That meant that all ethnic Germans outside the bor-ders of Germany ought to be ruled by Hitler, and conversely, that all "non-Germans" inside Germany were his enemies.

Foremost among those imaginary enemies were the Jews. Hit-ler blamed the Jews for everything that went wrong in Germany.

The Jews were behind Communism; the Jews were behind the economic depression; the Jews had conspired to make Germany lose the war. The survival of the German race depended on winning the undeclared war against the Jews.

That warped sense of patriotism was the only religion Hitler practiced. Hitler had been baptized a Catholic, but he believed that traditional religion was mere superstition: "Whether it is the Old Testament or the New, or simply the sayings of Jesus . . . it's all the same old Jewish swindle."[1] He seems to have believed in some sort of god, but his was a god who could appreciate strong fighters like himself, not a weakling god who would tell his followers to turn the other cheek.

However, Hitler kept those ideas to himself for a while. He and his Nazi Party promoted themselves as the defenders of old-fashioned morality and family values. And it was certainly true that there had been moral corruption in Germany—especially in Berlin, the most decadent city in Europe. So there were plenty of Christians—both Catholic and Protestant—who welcomed Hitler as a reformer. The Lutheran bishop of Württemberg, Theophil Wurm, was so pleased with Hitler's first few months in power that he wrote a letter in praise of Hitler to all his clergy. (He would later become one of Hitler's most outspoken critics, at least outside the concentration camps.)

Negotiating with the Devil

Pope Pius XI watched Hitler's rise with deep suspicion. Hitler's pious platitudes about morals and family life were appealing, but the pope wondered whether he could be trusted.

Before Hitler came to power, the Vatican had been negotiating a concordat with Germany—a treaty that would guarantee the rights of the Church in Germany in exchange for certain concessions. Now Hitler said he was willing to offer a very favorable agreement—more favorable than the previous German government would have accepted. The papal nuncio in charge of the negotiations, Cardinal Eugenio Pacelli, was not ready to trust Hitler. So Hitler pressured Pacelli by adding two additional "incentives" to sign the concordat. First, Hitler intimated that if the agreement were rejected, life might become very difficult for German Catholics—and he was perfectly capable of using any kind of terror to make this happen. Second, Hitler would release to the world the terms of the agreement he had offered, and the world would see how unreasonable the Church had been to reject them.

Cardinal Pacelli hated Nazism and everything it stood for, but he faced a tough dilemma. As he said later, "I had to choose between an agreement on their lines and the virtual elimination of the Catholic Church in the Reich." He told the British ambassador to the Vatican that "a pistol had been pointed at his head and he had no alternative."[2] And besides, as Pope Pius XI himself put it, "If it is a matter of saving a few souls, of averting even graver damage, we have the courage to negotiate even with the devil."[3]

Hitler, for his part, had made some very generous promises. The Church could keep its property and appoint its own bishops and priests, run its own schools, and establish seminaries. Most important, the Church won a concession on the increasingly oppressive race laws: a baptized Jew would be officially a German Christian. In days to come, false certificates of baptism would be important tools in the desperate race to save innocent Jews from the Nazi madness.

Hitler could afford to make as many promises as he liked, because he had no intention of keeping them. Cardinal Pacelli suspected as much. Nevertheless, he said to the French ambassador to the Vatican, "I do not regret our concordat with Germany. If we did not have it, we would not have a foundation on which to base our protests."[4] Besides, as the cardinal later said with a resigned smile, even the Nazis probably couldn't violate *all* the articles of the concordat at the same time.

THE NAZIS CONDEMNED

The concordat with Germany didn't mean that the pope approved of Hitler and Hitler's policies. On the contrary, it was necessary precisely because the Church was fundamentally opposed to Hitler's program, and Hitler knew it. Speaking in the plural to refer to himself, as was the Vatican custom at the time, Pope Pius XI wrote,

> Hence, despite many and grave misgivings, We then decided not to withhold Our consent, for We wished to spare the Faithful of Germany, as far as it was humanly possible, the trials and difficulties they would have had to face, given the circumstances, had the negotiations fallen through. It was by acts that We wished to make it plain, Christ's interests being Our sole object, that the pacific and maternal hand of the Church would be extended to anyone who did not actually refuse it.[5]

Those words came from an encyclical the pope wrote to the bishops of Germany in 1937. Most encyclicals are published in

Latin, but the pope thought it was vital for the German people to hear what he had to say. Thus this encyclical, *Mit Brennender Sorge* ("With Burning Anxiety"), was published first in German. It condemned the Nazi ideas of race and state in detail, and left no doubt that a Christian could not believe in the Nazi philosophy. The Nazis would never have let it be published, so it was smuggled into the country. On Palm Sunday these words were read from every Catholic pulpit in the land:

> Whoever exalts race, or the people, or the State, or a particular form of State, or the depositories of power, or any other fundamental value of the human community—however necessary and honorable be their function in worldly things—whoever raises these notions above their standard value and divinizes them to an idolatrous level, distorts and perverts an order of the world planned and created by God; he is far from the true faith in God and from the concept of life which that faith upholds. . . .
>
> None but superficial minds could stumble into concepts of a national God, of a national religion; or attempt to lock within the frontiers of a single people, within the narrow limits of a single race, God, the Creator of the universe, King and Legislator of all nations, before whose immensity they are "as a drop from a bucket" (Isaiah 40:15).[6]

Hitler's ideas of race and state were not the only problems the Church faced in Germany. If the Jews were the enemy, then nothing Jewish could be valuable or worthwhile. But since the Old Testament was Jewish, the Nazis ignored it altogether, thus promoting a new form of the ancient heresy Marcionism, which taught that Christianity was distinct from and in opposition to Judaism. Addressing this problem, the pope continued,

> Whoever wishes to see banished from church and school the biblical history and the wise doctrines of the Old Testament blasphemes the name of God, blasphemes the Almighty's plan of salvation, and makes limited and narrow human thought the judge of God's designs over the history of the world: he denies his faith in the true Christ, such as He appeared in the flesh, the Christ who took His human nature from a people that was to crucify Him; and he understands nothing of that universal tragedy of the Son of God who to His torturers' sacrilege opposed the divine and priestly sacrifice of His redeeming death, and made the new alliance the goal of the old alliance, its realization and its crown.

The Nazis were especially keen to impose their false ideas on the young. From a very early age, children were taught how to love the fatherland and hate Jews. In school, children recited a kind of parody of the Our Father in which they gave thanks to Hitler for their daily bread. So the pope had a few special words for the youth of Germany:

> Thousands of voices ring into your ears a Gospel which has not been revealed by the Father of Heaven. Thousands of pens are wielded in the service of a Christianity, which is not of Christ. Press and wireless daily force on you productions hostile to the Faith and to the Church, impudently aggressive against whatever you should hold

venerable and sacred. Many of you, clinging to your Faith and to your Church, as a result of your affiliation with religious associations guaranteed by the concordat, have often to face the tragic trial of seeing your loyalty to your country misunderstood, suspected, or even denied, and of being hurt in your professional and social life. We are well aware that there is many a humble soldier of Christ in your ranks, who with torn feelings, but a determined heart, accepts his fate, finding his one consolation in the thought of suffering insults for the name of Jesus (Acts 5:41). Today, as We see you threatened with new dangers and new molestations, We say to you: If any one should preach to you a Gospel other than the one you received on the knees of a pious mother, from the lips of a believing father, or through teaching faithful to God and His Church, "let him be anathema" (Galatians 1:9).[7]

Many of the Lutheran bishops and pastors went along with the Hitler's perversion of Christianity, although others died as martyrs in the concentration camps. The Nazis encouraged populist evangelists, who preached the new doctrine with plenty of lively music and stage effects, to whip up enthusiasm. One of the most important doctrines of the new "Christianity" was that no one whose ancestors were Jewish could be a pastor, and Christians of Jewish heritage had to have their own separate congregations.

Catholics could never reconcile the Nazi form of "Christianity" with the Catholic faith. The pope's encyclical put Hitler into a towering rage, and from then on he saw faithful Catholics as his enemies.

Pope Pius XI died less than two years after the publication of that encyclical (he had written it from his sickbed), but he lived long enough to see the situation turn from bad to worse. Mussolini aligned himself with Hitler, and Italy adopted the Nazi race philosophy, with all its repressive race laws, in 1938. Now the pope had good reason to regret having ever said that Mussolini had been sent by divine providence. The tiny Vatican state was surrounded by a Fascist power that was hostile to everything the Church stood for. The pope's protests against the new race laws were met by threats from Mussolini. But the Vatican's protests did have some impact in mostly Catholic Italy, where the race laws were only spottily enforced. Meanwhile, the pope met with the leaders of the democracies and urged them to deal with the rising tide of refugees. He also sent strongly worded instructions to North American Catholic universities to hire as many fleeing Jewish scholars as possible.

Pius XI died in February of 1939. As his successor, the cardinals chose Cardinal Eugenio Pacelli, the man who had negotiated the concordat with the Nazis; he took the name Pius XII. If the cardinals were hoping that Pacelli's diplomatic skill would come in handy over the next few years, they were right.

THE SCIENCE OF DEATH

Hitler spent the 1930s gradually extending his empire by iron-fisted diplomacy and carefully calculated shows of force. But the expansion wasn't moving fast enough for him. In September of 1939, the German army invaded Poland, launching the Second World War.

Some of the first victims of the German invasion in Poland were the priests. Cardinal Pacelli had been right: the Nazis couldn't violate every article of the concordat at once in Germany. But in conquered Poland, there was no need to pretend. The Nazis wanted to subdue the country as quickly as possible, and in a devoutly Catholic country like Poland, priests were the natural leaders of the people. "All Polish intelligentsia must be exterminated," wrote Hitler's private secretary. "This sounds cruel, but such is the law of life."[8] Therefore, the priests had to be eliminated.

No one knows how many priests were "exterminated." We know that three thousand priests died in concentration camps in Poland alone, along with more than five hundred monks, about three hundred nuns, and six bishops. No one can count how many lay believers went along with them, but it was probably about three million—about one Pole of every seven.

The Nazis intended ultimately to destroy the Polish race, but for the time being, their goal was for the Poles to be quiet and submissive. However, to Hitler the Jews were the primary enemy. And Hitler had decided that they must all die—every single one of them.

What can be said about a man who would destroy a whole race? Some have called Hitler a madman, but in fact he was horribly, monstrously sane. He knew exactly what he was doing, and with cold calculation spent years working out the most efficient way to do it. Christians have a word for what men like him do: evil. Of course, such a person seldom sees himself as doing evil. On the contrary, he is likely to believe that he alone understands what is good. "I believe that I am doing the will of the Almighty Creator," Hitler wrote. "By defending myself against the Jew, I am fighting for the work of the Lord."[9]

Of the Christians who died in Nazi concentration camps,

many of them were condemned for the simple crime of trying to save a Jew's life. When Pius XII heard of the invasion, he fell on his knees and prayed for a long time. Then he had thousands of baptismal certificates drafted and made ready to help Jews escape to safety. Throughout the Nazi occupation, Catholic leaders would work with the Polish underground to rescue as many Jews as they could. But they were working against the most efficient system of organized murder ever devised.

Wherever the Nazis took over, they began rounding up the Jews and "relocating" them—in reality sending them off to death camps to be worked to death or simply killed outright. In Holland, which the Nazis had also conquered, the Catholic bishops protested strongly from the pulpits against the treatment of the Jews there. The result was that the Nazis also decided to round up Catholics of "Jewish blood." The protest had made the situation even more dangerous. It was a lesson the new pope would have to remember as he tried to deal with the Nazi horror.

The numbers of Jews who died—murdered by Nazis for the "purification" of Europe—are simply staggering. Again, no one has an exact count. The most likely figure is about six million. And more than just the people themselves died. A whole culture, with centuries of tradition, was destroyed.

All this death was made possible by a carefully planned system that allowed each concentration camp to murder and dispose of thousands of victims each day. It had all been worked out and tested on Germans—Germans who were in some way considered "defective." Children who had birth defects or had developmental disabilities, and eventually even children with simple problems like bed-wetting were rounded up and sent to gas chambers. To the Nazis, these lives weren't worth anything anyway, and getting rid of such people made the German race stronger. When the news leaked out about the program to exterminate Germans who were considered "imperfect," a wave of protest swept through Germany. But the Nazis weathered it, and the extermination went on.

THE "PRO-JEWISH POPE"

As the war continued, Pope Pius XII found himself in a troublesome position. He declared neutrality, but he couldn't really be neutral about the Nazi atrocities. Hitler and the Nazis considered him a mortal enemy. Hitler angrily called him "this pro-Jewish Pope."[10]

On the other hand, though his sympathies were with the Allies, the pope could hardly make his sympathies public. Although the Vatican was independent, it was surrounded by Italy, and the pope knew that if he went too far the Fascists might take away his power to do any good at all. Hitler had threatened several times to bomb the Vatican. Workmen were busy digging bomb shelters—not for the pope, since he refused to go into a shelter, but for the priceless manuscripts and art treasures of the Vatican.

In spite of the pope's public neutrality, the Vatican Radio continued to broadcast intense criticisms of the Nazis. German officials who complained were told that the Jesuits ran the Vatican Radio as a separate enterprise. But many years after the war, it came to light that many of the most aggressively anti-Nazi broadcasts had been written by Pius himself.

Still, the public face of neutrality had to be maintained. Even the Vatican Radio had to be more restrained than the pope would have liked. When the Vatican Radio made an appeal to Poles to resist religious oppression, the result was death by torture for hundreds of Polish priests. And the Vatican could not ignore the fact that most of the nations allied with or conquered by Hitler were Catholic.

The Vatican's neutrality also gave it access to the conquered territories. It was the Vatican that first brought the world the news of the Nazi atrocities against Jews in Poland and in Germany itself. The government of the United States at the time refused to believe the reports until there was more evidence, but the Vatican's sources had provided correct information.

Pius XII sent his nuncio in Germany to Hitler to protest the atrocities personally, but the meeting was not successful. "He turned his back on me and started to drum on the glass with his fingers," the nuncio, Cesare Orsenigo, reported. "All of a sudden, Hitler turned around, grabbed a glass off a nearby table, and hurled it to the floor with an angry gesture. Faced with this kind of diplomatic behavior, I thought my mission was over."[11]

THE GREAT RESCUE

In 1941, two separate events changed the course of the war. First, the Germans invaded Russia without warning. Second, the sudden Japanese attack on Pearl Harbor pushed the United States into the war.

At first, the Nazi invasion of Russia appeared to be a success. But the stubborn resistance of the Russians delayed the invasion long enough for winter to set in, and Russian winters are usually fatal to invaders. Hitler had planned a quick conquest of the Soviet Union. If he had succeeded, the war might have ended very differently. Instead, he found his troops mired in an increasingly hopeless invasion to the east, while the entry of the United States made it improbable that Britain would eventually accept a peace on Hitler's terms.

Millions of Americans went off to fight in Europe and the Pacific. The entire country got behind the war, with men fighting on the front lines and women and even children working at home to support the war effort. By 1943 the tide had definitely turned in favor of the Allies. Italy was crumbling. The US president, Franklin Delano Roosevelt, who was in constant contact with the pope, suggested that Pius should tell Italians it was time to get rid of Mussolini. The pope sent a message to the king of Italy, who was largely a figurehead but still had theoretical power, along with the Grand Council, to depose Mussolini. On July 24 Mussolini got the bad news from the king. Then he was taken away by secret police.[12]

Hitler was furious. He blamed the pope for the change of governments in Italy, and he didn't trust the new government to stay on his side. He was right: in September Italy switched sides and joined the Allies. But Hitler had already made his move. German forces took over northern Italy, including Rome, and now the pope was surrounded by Nazis. Hitler was even threatening to kidnap the pope the way Napoléon had done.

But there was an even more pressing problem. Until this time, the Jews in Italy had been relatively safe. Now the Germans were determined to enforce the race laws to the letter, and deportations began. Faced with this emergency, the pope ordered every religious institution to open its doors to Jewish refugees. In Rome itself, about a third of the Jewish population took refuge in buildings belonging to the Church. Catholic hospitals took in Jewish "patients" who weren't sick at all.

The Church mobilized all its forces. "No hero in history has commanded such an army," wrote Israel Zolli, the chief rabbi of Rome. "An army of priests works in cities and small towns to provide bread for the persecuted and passports for the refugees."[13] Zolli himself was one of the thousands who found refuge with the Church in Rome, although he had offered himself to the Nazis as a hostage in exchange for the release of other Jews.

Wherever the Church owned property, Pope Pius sheltered the Jewish refugees. And he meant to defend them to the last. No more was the Swiss Guard a ceremonial force in colorful uniforms. Now they had machine guns, and they stood guard over every building where the Jews were sheltered. The pope even had his seal carved on the entrance to the Great Synagogue in Rome, marking it as Vatican territory. Meanwhile, thousands of blank baptismal certificates and other documents were sent to the Jews of Italy. The concordat with Germany paid off: German soldiers usually left alone those Jews who had supposedly converted. The pope himself ordered that clerical clothing be handed out to many of the Jews so that they could disguise themselves as priests.

Many Catholic priests died for the crime of sheltering Jews. But many other priests were never caught, and thousands upon thousands of refugees survived because of the Church.

Finally, on June 4, 1944, the Allies reached Rome. The Germans had threatened to destroy the city rather than give it up, but in fact they left quietly. The whole city erupted in joy. The refugees who had been in hiding all this time poured into St. Peter's Square and celebrated.

Later, the American general who led the invading army

stopped to see the pope. "I am afraid you have been disturbed by the noise of my tanks," he told Pope Pius. "I am sorry."

The pope smiled broadly. "General," he replied, "any time you come to liberate Rome, you can make just as much noise as you like."[14]

All over the world, Jewish leaders sent their thanks to the Holy Father for his work in saving so many Italian Jews from the death camps. "The Catholic Church saved more Jewish lives during the war than all other churches, religious institutions, and rescue organizations put together," wrote Israel's consul in Italy. "The Holy See, the nuncios, and the entire Catholic Church saved some eight hundred thousand Jews from certain death."[15] The World Jewish Congress donated about twenty thousand dollars to Vatican charities in thanks for the pope's rescue efforts. One Jewish leader went even further. Rabbi Zolli, the chief rabbi who had taken refuge in Vatican property along with those many thousands of other Jews in Rome, was struck to the heart by the Christian charity he had seen. He was baptized as a Catholic, and he took the Christian name Eugenio, in honor of Eugenio Pacelli, Pope Pius XII.

A Closer Look . . .

"I Want to Take His Place"

Maximilian Kolbe was a Catholic priest sent to Auschwitz by the Nazis. No one knows for sure how many prisoners died at that horrible concentration camp, but estimates run to as many as three million. Some of the victims were killed outright. Others starved to death or died of overwork. And some, of course, tried to escape.

The Nazis had a particularly brutal way of dealing with escapes. For every prisoner who escaped, they would kill ten of the prisoners who remained. And those ten victims wouldn't die immediately—instead, they'd be locked in a room and slowly starved to death.

One time when the guards couldn't find one of the prisoners, they rounded up the usual ten victims.

"My poor wife! My poor children!" one of the victims cried. "What will they do?"

Of course, the commandant expected scenes like that. What he did not expect was what happened next. Suddenly there was a prisoner standing in front of him, his cap off, making a respectful request.

"I'm a priest," the prisoner said. "Let me take his place. I'm old, but he has a wife and children."

The commandant couldn't believe his ears. He had to ask the prisoner to repeat what he had said.

"I'm a Polish priest," Fr. Kolbe repeated. "I want to take his place, because he has a wife and children."

The commandant had never heard such a request. But it was fine with him if the priest wanted to die instead of the young worker, who might still be useful around the camp.

So, Fr. Kolbe gave up his life for a man he hardly knew. That man, whose name was Francis Gajowniczek, survived the war and lived many years after—long enough to see the canonization of St. Maximilian Kolbe. And he never stopped telling the world what the great saint and martyr had done.[16]

11

The History of the Future

With the end of the Second World War, we reach the modern age—the era in which we or our parents grew up. We often think of history as what happened before we were born, consisting of stories that are very remote from us. But history continues through our own age into the future, and it always follows the same broad patterns.

Cardinal John Henry Newman showed us how to understand even our own history. History, he said, is "a circle ever enlarging."[1] Former events were "types" or patterns of the events of our own time, and what happens now is a type of what will happen in the future. In the fourth century, the Church struggled over the interpretation and application of the controversial Council of Nicea—a glorious council whose canons were badly misused over the subsequent decades. In the 1960s, Pope John XXIII would startle the world by summoning a council to address the evangelization of the modern world. We should not be surprised that the council's aftermath produced great spiritual fruit, such as the rise of new apostolic and spiritual movements in the Church and progress in ecumenism, but also some unintended and destructive outcomes, including a rebellion against Church authority and an exodus from the ranks of the priesthood and religious life.

The Council of Renewal

In the 1950s, Pope Pius XII had considered summoning a council of the world's bishops, and he even drafted preliminary plans for the event. He concluded, however, that the time was not right. Just a few years would make all the difference, as Pius's successor, Pope John XXIII, took up the plans once again. When he opened the Second Vatican Council in 1962, Pope John told the assembled delegates that he had called the council to protect the "sacred deposit" of Christian doctrine and to expound it more effectively in the modern world. Although the council would have the duty of rendering that doctrine more comprehensible to the current age, its primary duty would be to remain faithful to the centuries of tradition that were the foundation of that doctrine.

But the council had other important goals, and those made it the most talked-about event in modern Catholic history. First, the council was to work on nothing less than the spiritual renewal of the Church—a phrase pregnant with promise, but one that could easily be misinterpreted. Second, the council had a duty to bring the message of the Catholic Church to the world at large, including both non-Catholic Christians and non-Christians. Although there had been important contacts between Catholics and Protestants before, this was the real beginning of the ecumenical movement in the Church.

The council also called for renewal of Catholic Scripture study, clergy formation, and liturgy. It was this last area—liturgy—that would lead to the developments most visible to Catholics, as the outward rites of the Mass underwent their most thorough and sudden revision in the Church's history. The revision was so swift that it proved exhilarating for some, traumatic for others. The liturgy of the western Church had long been fairly uniform; but, after the council, the Church provided many new, optional texts, and left the choice of those texts to the priest-celebrant. For centuries in the West, the standard liturgical language had been Latin; after the council, the liturgies were translated into the vernacular languages, and soon Latin was hardly used at all.

Vatican II was the first Church council to face the immediate and intensive scrutiny of the electronic media. The rarefied debates of the bishops were almost daily reduced to bite-size reports and then broadcast the world over on the evening news. Bishop John Wright of Pittsburgh recalled the difficulty this presented:

Lou Cassels was among the most conscientious of the newsmen covering the Council. One afternoon it was my fell destiny to be assigned to help out at the American bishops' press conference. Lou put up his hand to ask clarification of the doctrine of the collegiality of the apostles and their successors, which had been discussed in the morning Council session. I tried to provide a brief summary of the scriptural exegesis, the theological interpretations, and the canonical developments, not to mention the heretical aberrations, on this knotty point throughout nineteen centuries of fierce speculation and activity surrounding it. When I finished— alas, a little vaingloriously—my twenty-minute attempt at a synthesis of the thoughts and actions of the centuries, Lou looked desperate and said: "How the heck do you compress all that into a five-hundred-word cable that must be in New York by five o'clock this afternoon?"[2]

It was a very good question. It also pointed out the problem that would face the bishops as they attempted to implement the decisions of the council in their own dioceses. The Second Vatican Council had taken years to formulate its conclusions. But many of the people at home knew only what they had read in five-hundred-word dispatches, many of them from less conscientious reporters than Lou Cassels. How could a bishop guard against misinterpretations of the council, but at the same time bring its riches home to his flock?

Pope John XXIII died less than a year after convening the council. The cardinals chose Cardinal Giovanni Montini to succeed him, and the new pope took the name Paul. True to the late Pope John's idea that a better understanding of the gospel was the key, the council began to rethink some of the most important questions that faced the Church. The result was not any change in doctrine, but instead an amplification of the eternal truths preserved by the Church and a new presentation of those truths for the modern age.

The role of the laity was one of the most important topics, and therefore one that provoked much debate. The council reminded Christians that priests, monks, and nuns are not the only people responsible for the spread of the gospel. "Upon all the laity, therefore, rests the noble duty of working to extend the divine plan of salvation to all men of each epoch and in every land. Consequently, may every opportunity be given them so that, according to their abilities and the needs of the times, they may zealously participate in the saving work of the Church."[3] These words signaled a powerful movement of the Spirit, which would give life to many existing apostolates and institutions and would inspire the formation of new ones. In the decade after the council, the worldwide Church would grow increasingly aware of the work and witness of the Catholic Charismatic Renewal, Communion and Liberation, Cursillo, Focolare, the Neo-Catechumenal Way, Opus Dei, Regnum Christi, Sant'Egidio, and many others. As these movements and spiritual families experienced new or renewed vigor from the council, they would serve as important heralds of its message in the difficult decades ahead.

The Red Menace

Many people alive today can remember a time when the "Red Menace" was an obsession. After the Second World War, the Communists grabbed more than half of Europe and ruthlessly suppressed any institution that competed with their totalitarian rule, especially the Church.

Millions of perceived enemies of the state were imprisoned in concentration camps. Trainloads of Catholics were sent to Siberia (where today there are thriving Catholic communities). Massacre and genocide were simply matters of policy.

Millions of prayers went up to heaven from those Communist prison camps, and for a while it must have seemed as though God was deaf to them. But God always raises up the deliverers we need. God answered those prayers in a way that would reflect his glory and result in the greater good of all his people. Just as he raised up Gregory at the onset of the Dark Ages, he raised up John Paul II to be a light in the darkness of Communist oppression.

John Paul was in every way an extraordinary man. He was a world-famous philosopher as well as a religious leader. As a layman, Karol Wojtyla had been a poet and an actor in the Polish theater. He was also a perfect pope for his era. Here was a man who grew up in a single-parent household (his mother died when he was eight years old), who labored in quarries and chemical factories, who survived the Nazi occupation of Poland, who worked his way through school, who enjoyed the theater and the ski slopes, who could kick a soccer ball and loved to dance, who knew the friendship of atheists and agnostics, and who played the guitar. This was not a remote bureaucrat, or a mere liturgical functionary, or a faceless cleric who spent his life running the obstacle course of Church politics. John Paul II was one of us.

The Catholic world rejoiced at the election, but the feeling in Poland was indescribable. Wojtyla was someone who, as a prelate in Poland, had resisted the might of the Communists. Instead of being crushed by them, he had risen through the ranks of the Church and had been elected by his fellow cardinals to be pope. Before this momentous event, it had seemed useless to resist the Communists actively, but now there was hope. Not long after John Paul was elected to the chair of Peter, the Polish people launched their struggle to overthrow the Communists. It took more than a decade, but it happened. And once Poland was free, Communist governments fell like dominoes all over Europe. By the end of John Paul's papacy, only Cuba and North Korean had not given up on Communism, while China and Vietnam had modified their Communism to incorporate elements of capitalism, but still remained intensely hostile to Christianity.

When John Paul II died in 2005, membership in the Catholic Church was larger than it had ever been in history, and it was growing at a healthy rate. It appeared that the Church had triumphed over the crises of the past century. Yet plenty of people believed that the Church was a relic of the past, soon to fade away into the footnotes of history books.

The Latest Crisis

It was certainly true that the Church faced some challenges. In America, the Church found itself opposing certain emerging cultural trends: the gradual acceptance, for example, of contraception, abortion, euthanasia, divorce, and homosexual activity. In some states, legislation made it increasingly difficult for parishes to sustain Catholic schools. And the popular media kept up what can only be called a full-scale assault on the Church, with pop entertainment portraying priests as hypocritical fanatics and the faithful as hopelessly naïve.

As if that weren't enough, a heartbreaking scandal erupted over charges of pedophilia by priests in dioceses across the country. Lawsuits filed by victims of sexual abuse drove some dioceses into bankruptcy amid allegations that bishops knew of the abuses but covered them up. The scandal brought the relentless media spotlight on the Church, and priests became the butt of crude jokes daily on talk radio and late-night television. Oddly enough, in one way, the scandal only served to reinforce the Church's timeless teaching that we are all susceptible to sin—even priests.

To prevent such scandals from happening in the future, diocesan policies and procedures were implemented throughout the country. The Catholic Church, especially in the United States, was the first large organization to address the problem of sexual abuse in a comprehensive and practical way. These policies and procedures now provide a working model for other organizations that deal with children.

Still, the combination of shameful scandal and cultural hostility sometimes made it a grim time to be Catholic.

Americans tend to be myopic and see the Church only through

the lens of their own nation. But the Church in America makes up only a small fraction of a billion people who belong to the Catholic Church all over the world. Millions of Catholics live on every continent, and in some of those places the Church is growing at an amazing rate. Now Africa and Asia are exporting priests to parishes in the United States, as many American Catholics have been delighted to discover. The Church is more truly "catholic" now than at any time in history.

So what is the real story of the Church in the twenty-first century?

No one could deny that the Church is facing a crisis. But that's nothing new. If we've learned anything from the past two thousand years, it's that the Church is always facing a crisis.

In fact, as the historian Philip Jenkins points out, crises are what drive the Church. "The best indicator that Christianity is about to experience a vast expansion is a widespread conviction that the religion is doomed or in its closing days."[4] Over and over again, the doubters have confidently predicted the end of the Church, only to be overwhelmed at the next moment by a sudden burst of Christian energy.

In the early part of the twentieth century, G. K. Chesterton noticed the same phenomenon:

Christianity has died many times and risen again; for it had a God who knew the way out of the grave. But the first extraordinary fact which marks this history is this: that Europe has been turned upside down over and over again; and that at the end of each of these revolutions the same religion has again been found on top. The Faith is always converting the age, not as an old religion but as a new religion."[5]

The pagan Romans thought the Christians would just go away if they passed laws that were strict enough. Instead, that odd little Jewish sect conquered the empire.

The Arians rationalized the central mysteries of Christianity away, and confidently celebrated their victory. Instead, orthodox Christianity triumphed, and the Arians faded into history.

In the High Middle Ages, heresies and intellectual skepticism seemed ready to make the Church a shell of empty rituals. Instead, the age brought forth both some of the greatest theologians and the greatest mystics in Christian history.

In the Renaissance, the revival of pagan learning and taste threatened to reduce the Church to a crusty old irrelevance. Instead, the same age saw an explosive growth of the Church in all four corners of the world.

The French Revolution, and the secularist revolutions throughout Europe in the 1800s, took away the temporal power of the Church and seemed to threaten the extinction of the whole institution. Instead, there was a great religious revival all over the world, one whose effects we're still feeling today.

The Communists ruled half of Europe and most of Asia for half a century, and it may have seemed that the Church was wiped out in both continents. Instead, it was Christians, led by a pope from a Communist country, who overthrew the Communists. The Church remains, still doing the work it did in secret for fifty years.

Now, as countless dozen pundits confidently predict the end of Christianity and the beginning of a new, "post-Christian" age, we can predict, if only from the example of history, that they'll be wrong. The Church will find new energy, and the billion faithful will stay true to what they believe. Even when we suffer with Jesus, we know that we also rise with Jesus.

"We are afflicted in every way, but not crushed; perplexed, but not driven to despair; persecuted, but not forsaken; struck down, but not destroyed; always carrying in the body the death of Jesus, so that the life of Jesus may also be made visible in our bodies" (2 Corinthians 4:8-10).

This is as true of the whole Church as it is of the individual Christian. This is why the orant figure—the "praying person" we described in our introduction—is always shown standing, and is still standing after all these centuries.

THE ENDURING TRUTH

So here we are, back at the beginning. Two thousand years have passed since the birth of the Church. The world is different, and the Church is different, in countless ways. But in the most important ways, nothing has changed. The Church still proclaims the message of the gospel, which is timeless and perfect. The structure of the Church has been refined to fit current conditions, and it will be refined more when more refining is needed. But the fundamental structure will always be the same. The successors of the apostles will always guide the Church, with the successor of Peter as their head.

The pagan Roman Empire is long gone, but the world still persecutes the Church, overtly in some places, more subtly in others. Martyrs still die for the Christian faith every year, and the blood of the martyrs still makes the Church stronger.

Christ's promise is still good: he is always with his Church, "to the end of the age" (Matthew 28:20). The world can dismiss the Church as outmoded, irrelevant, a fading dinosaur. But the

Church will always be new. In the end, the latest fashion in secular philosophy, whatever it is today, will join Theophilanthropism on the forgotten back shelves of history. Christianity will be the latest thing, the newest revolution, the will of the people.

So what will archaeologists of the future find when they dig down to the remains of the twenty-first century?

Just as archaeologists do today with the remains from two thousand years ago, they'll find all the things we didn't think much about at the time. They'll find city neighborhoods where almost every house has a plastic statue of the Virgin Mary in its backyard. They'll find millions of little medals with images of saints. Crosses and crucifixes will fill the basement drawers of their museums. They'll find churches in every neighborhood. And everywhere they'll see Christian symbols—the cross, the fish, the loaves and the grapes, and the praying hands.

Those future archaeologists will read the secular literature of the twenty-first century with all its dire predictions: the Church won't last another century, it has to change or die, no one believes that stuff anymore. They'll turn to their overflowing drawers of crucifixes and smile. They'll know the real story, the one that was so obvious, right out in the open, but not discussed by the secular culture. They'll shake their heads and wonder how those ancient writers could have been so blind.

Then they'll close their museum drawers and go to Mass.

Notes

Introduction (pp. 7–12)

1. Graydon F. Snyder, *Ante Pacem: Archaeological Evidence of Church Life Before Constantine* (Macon, GA: Mercer University, 2003), 36.

2. See, for example, St. Athanasius, *On the Incarnation of the Word*, 8; St. Cyril of Alexandria, *Commentary on John* 14:20, 11. In using the Church Fathers, I have often consulted multiple translations as well as the originals, whenever possible. Some quotations are new translations; some are composites where I have exercised editorial judgment, drawing from varied translations. In all cases, I have tried to achieve maximum clarity and fidelity to the sense of the originals.

3. Leo XIII, *Saepenumero Considerantes* (Letter on Historical Studies), delivered on the opening of the Vatican Archives, August 18, 1883.

4. Augustine, *City of God*, 20.9, quoted in Scott Hahn and Mike Aquilina, *Living the Mysteries* (Huntington, IN: 2003), 195–97.

1. The Martyr's Cup (pp. 13–26)

1. Tacitus, *Annals,* 15.44.

2. Tacitus, *Annals,* 15.44.

3. See Rodney Stark, *The Rise of Christianity* (San Francisco: HarperCollins, 1997), 7.

4. Justin Martyr, *Dialogue with Trypho,* 41.

5. Ignatius of Antioch, *Epistle to the Romans,* 4.

6. *Martyrdom of Polycarp,* 15.

7. *Acts of Pionius,* 21, quoted in Herbert Musurillo, *Acts of the Christian Martyrs* (New York: Oxford, 1972), 163.

8. *The Martyrdom of Saint Irenaeus Bishop of Sirmium,* quoted in Herbert Musurillo, *Acts of the Christian Martyrs,* 295.

9. See Robin Darling Young, *In Procession Before the World: Martyrdom as Public Liturgy in Early Christianity* (Milwaukee: Marquette University Press, 2001).

10. Jerome, *De Persecutione Christianorum,* quoted in Boniface Ramsey, *Beginning to Read the Fathers* (Mahwah, NJ: Paulist, 1985), 133.

11. Tertullian, *Apologeticum,* 39.7.

12. Eusebius, *Church History,* 1.25.

13. Tertullian, *Apologeticum,* 1.

14. Irenaeus, *Adversus Haereses,* 3.3.2.

15. Theodoret, Letter to Pope Leo.

16. Leo the Great, Sermon, 82.1.

17. Justin Martyr, *Dialogue with Trypho,* 100.

2. The Case for Christianity (pp. 27–38)

1. Justin Martyr, *Dialogue with Trypho,* 100.

2. Justin Martyr, *Dialogue with Trypho,* 8.

3. Justin Martyr, *First Apology,* 67.

4. Stark, *Rise of Christianity,* 118.

5. Dionysius of Alexandria, quoted in Stark, *Rise of Christianity,* 82.

6. Dionysius, quoted in Stark, *Rise of Christianity,* 84.

7. Eusebius, *On the Life of Constantine,* 1.28.

8. Eusebius, *Ecclesiastical History,* 9.9.11.

3. Heresy and Orthodoxy (pp. 39–52)

1. Jerome, *Dialogue Against the Luciferians* 19.
2. Augustine, *Confessions,* 1.1.

4. Light in the Dark Ages (pp. 53–66)

1. Cassiodorus, *Institutions,* 30
2. Cassiodorus, *Institutions,* 30.
3. Bede, *Ecclesiastical History,* 2.1.
4. Bede, *Ecclesiastical History,* 1.23.
5. Bede, *Ecclesiastical History,* 1.27.
6. Patrick, *Confession,* 1.16.

5. Crusades Abroad and at Home (pp. 67–84)

1. Nasir-I Khusraw, quoted in F. E. Peters, *Jerusalem* (Princeton, NJ: Princeton University, 1985), 244, 267.
2. Adapted from *The Little Flowers of St. Francis,* http://penelope.uchicago.edu/Thayer/E/Gazetteer/People/Francis_of_Assisi/_Texts/Fioretti/16.html.

6. Reformation Inside and Out (pp. 85–98)

1. Martin Luther, *Against King Henry of England.*
2. Roper, *Life of Sir Thomas More,* included in *The Utopia of Sir Thomas More* (Roslyn, NY: Walter J. Black, 1947), 280.
3. Calvin, *Institutes,* 3.21.7.
4. Benedict Zimmerman, OCD, Introduction to St. John of the Cross, *Spiritual Canticle* [1909], Electronic Edition with Modernization of English by Harry Plantinga, http://www.ccel.org/ccel/john_cross/canticle.ii.html, 1995.

7. The Conversion of the New World (pp. 99–110)

1. Las Casas, *Destruction of the Indies,* Preface.
2. Las Casas, *Destruction of the Indies,* xx.
3. Las Casas, *Destruction of the Indies,* xx.
4. Cortés, Letter 2, ch. 5.
5. Recent archaeological finds corroborate the pre-Columbian Aztec traditions. See Mark Stevenson, "Evidence May Back Human Sacrifice Claims," Associated Press, January 23, 2005.
6. Cortés, Letter 2, ch. 5.
7. The story is found in the *Nican Mopohua of Don Antonio Valeriano*; it appears online in English translation at http://www.interlupe.com.mx/4-e.html.
8. Voltaire, *Essai sur les moeurs et l'esprit des nations,* 154.
9. Quoted in "The Suppression of the Jesuits," *Catholic Encyclopedia,* http://www.newadvent.org/cathen/14096a.htm.

8. The World Goes Mad (pp. 111–28)

1. Rousseau, *Discourse on Inequality,* 2.
2. Browning, ed., *The Despatches of Earl Gower, English Ambassador at Paris from June 1790 to August 1792* (Cambridge: Cambridge University, 1885).
3. Quoted in M. A. Thiers, *History of the French Revolution,* vol. 2, (Philadelphia: Carey and Hart, 1842), 370–71.
4. Napoléon Bonaparte, quoted in John Henry Newman, *Certain Difficulties Felt by Anglicans in Catholic Teaching,* vol. 2 (London: Longmans, Green, 1900), 215.
5. Quoted in Clare Boothe Luce. ed., *Saints for Now* (New York: Sheed & Ward, 1952), 278.

6. Bruce Marshall, *The Curé of Ars,* http://www.cin.org/
saints/curears-marshall.html.

7. Premier edition of *The Pittsburgh Catholic* newspaper,
March 16, 1844, front page.

8. P. J. Mahon and J. M. Hayes, eds., *Trials and Triumphs of
the Catholic Church in America* (Chicago: J. S. Hyland, 1907),
732.

9. Mahon and Hayes, *Trials and Triumphs,* ch. 33.

10. Francis A. Glenn, *Shepherds of the Faith* (Pittsburgh:
Diocese of Pittsburgh, 1993), 67.

9. The Secular Age (pp. 129–40)

1. The story was reported and corroborated by several
members of Pope Leo's household. Pope John Paul II confirmed
the major details in his *Regina Coeli* address of April 24, 1994.

2. Patricia O'Connor, *Thérèse of Lisieux* (Huntington, IN:
Our Sunday Visitor, 1984), p. 87.

3. St. Thérèse of Lisieux, *Story of a Soul: The Autobiography
of St. Therese of Lisieux,* trans. John Clarke, OCD
(Washington, DC: ICS Publications, 1976), 207.

4. Dorothy Day, *Thérèse* (Notre Dame, IN: Fides, 1960), xii.

5. *Grace in Every Season: Through the Year with Catherine
Doherty,* ed. Mary Achterhoff (Ann Arbor, MI: Servant Books,
1992), 241.

6. Josemaría Escrivá, *Camino,* 402 (Spanish edition only).

10. A Century of Cataclysms (pp. 141–58)

1. Adolph Hitler, quoted in Ambrus Miskolczy, *Hitler's
Library* (Budapest: Central European University Press, 2003), 25.

2. Eugenio Pacelli, quoted in Ronald J. Rychlak, *Hitler, the*

War, and the Pope (Huntington, IN: Our Sunday Visitor), 58.

3. Rychlak, *Hitler,* 59.

4. Rychlak, *Hitler,* 60.

5. Pius XI, *Mit Brennender Sorge,* 3, http://www.vatican
.va/holy_father/pius_xi/encyclicals/documents/hf_p-xi_enc_
14031937_mit-brennender-sorge_en.html.

6. Pius XI, *Mit Brennender Sorge,* 8, 11.

7. Pius XI, *Mit Brennender Sorge,* 32–33.

8. Pius XI, *Mit Brennender Sorge,* 121.

9. Adolph Hitler, *Mein Kampf* (New York: Houghton
Mifflin, 1969), 60.

10. Margherita Marchione, *Consensus and Controversy*
(Mawhah, NJ: Paulist, 2002), 112.

11. Rychlak, *Hitler,* 184.

12. Rychlak, *Hitler,* 198–99.

13. Eugenio Zolli, "The Charity of Pope Pius XII," excerpt
from his autobiography *Before the Dawn,* published in *Inside
the Vatican,* February 1999, 82–83.

14. Rychlak, *Hitler,* 217.

15. Pinchas E. Lapide, longtime Israeli consul in Italy,
quoted in Rychlak, *Hitler,* 240, 404, n. 9.

16. The story of St. Maximilian Kolbe is told in many
good books. Perhaps the most unusual—and fascinating—is
Ladislaus Kluz, *Kolbe and the Kommandant: Two Worlds
in Collision* (Stevenson, MT: Desmet, 1983), which is a dual
biography of the saint and Rudolf Hoess, the officer who
commanded the Auschwitz death camp during Kolbe's last
days. After the war, Hoess was imprisoned and sentenced to
death for his crimes. Awaiting his execution, he returned to the
Catholic faith of his childhood. Other excellent portraits are

Andre Frossard, *Forget Not Love: The Passion of Maximilian Kolbe* (San Francisco: Ignatius, 1991) and Boniface Hanley, OFM, *No Greater Love* (Notre Dame, IN: Ave Maria, 1982). The latter includes many photographs of the saint and other characters in the story.

11. The History of the Future (pp. 159–69)

1. John Henry Newman, *Discussions and Arguments on Various Subjects* (London: Longmans, Green, 1907), 49.

2. John Wright, "Conciliar Rome," in *Resonare Christum*, vol. 2 (San Francisco: Ignatius, 1988), 392–93.

3. Vatican Council II, *Lumen Gentium*, 33, http://www .vatican.va/archive/hist_councils/ii_vatican_council/documents /vat-ii_const_19641121_lumen-gentium_en.html.

4. Philip Jenkins, "Downward, Outward, Later," *Books and Culture*, September–October 2006, 10.

5. G. K. Chesterton, *The Everlasting Man* (New York: Dodd, Mead, 1926), 312.

Made in the USA
Coppell, TX
21 July 2021